D0409648

ES

HACKNEY AND STOKE NEWINGTON PAST

First published 1990
Revised editions 1998 and 2006
Historical Publications Ltd
32 Ellington Street, London N7 8PL
(Tel: 020 7607 1628)

© **Isobel Watson, 1990, 1998 and 2006**
The moral right of the author has been asserted
All rights reserved, unauthorised duplication contravenes applicable laws

ISBN 0 948667 54 0
British Library Cataloguing-in-Publication Data
A catalogue record for this book is available from the British Library

Typeset in Palatino by Historical Publications Ltd
Reproduction by G & J Graphics, London EC2
Printed by Edelvives, Zaragoza, Spain

HACKNEY AND STOKE NEWINGTON PAST

A visual history
of Hackney
and Stoke Newington

by
Isobel Watson

HISTORICAL PUBLICATIONS

Acknowledgements

This book owes a great deal to the consistent co-operation and advice, on miscellaneous enquiries over several years, of the staff of Hackney Archives Department, notably David Mander and Jean Wait, from whose depth and breadth of knowlege of the area I have learnt much. In particular, special thanks are owed to David for his comments on the first edition text in manuscript, and much valuable advice as to the contents of the Department's remarkable and ever-growing visual collection. I am also grateful to the staff of other record offices and repositories to which my researches have led me, notably the London Metropolitan Archives, the City and Hackney Health Authority, the National Portrait Gallery, the Prints and Drawings departments of the Museum of London, the British Museum and the Guildhall Library.

The text draws both on the sources mentioned below as further reading, on research published in *East London Papers*, the *East London Record*, the *Hackney Terrier* and *Hackney History*, and on new research. Since publication of the first edition, much good new work has been done, and the opportunity has been taken to add supplementary material and make corrections. The major event for Hackney history of all time has been the long-awaited volume X of the *Victoria County History of Middlesex*. And apart from the continuing work at the Archives (where David Mander has, amongst many other things, assisted me by correcting a former misattribution of illustration 39) there has been the opportunity to draw on Mike Gray's exhaustive research into the origins of Sutton House, and on information supplied in correspondence by D.B. Ballance, Dr Anita McConnell, Alan Ruston and Anne Wilkinson. A copy annotating the sources, including much lively newspaper material originating in the Tyssen library, is deposited with Hackney Archives Department.

But the book would not be what it is without the marvellous work undertaken, mostly in a single decade, the 1840s, by a handful of skilled and prescient artists concerned to record what was soon to be lost. Of these special mention shold be made of C.H. Matthews, Thomas Dibdin, George Hawkins, G. Toussaint, Charles Bigot and, last but never least, Thomas Hosmer Shepherd.

The Illustrations

Almost all the illustrations come from the collection of the Archives Department of the London Borough of Hackney, to whom we are most grateful for their enthusiastic co-operation. We would also like to thank the following for the use of other illustrations:

Frick Reference Library, New York: *170*
Guildhall Library, London: *52, 108, 142*
London Metropolitan Archives: *82, 139, 180*
MBC Publications: *182*
Museum of London: *93*
National Portrait Gallery: *176*

Illustrations *2, 22, 26, 27, 28, 30, 36, 37, 90, 91, 96, 149, 168, 169, 172, 173, 175, 176, 177, 178* were supplied by the publisher.

The jacket illustration is of Spring Lane, Clapton, by C. Bigot, *c.*1840.

Waltham Forest Libraries

904 000 00277319	
Askews & Holts	23-Aug-2013
942.144 WAT	£15.95
4002951	∟

Contents

Further Reading

Until recently most local historical material dated from the 19th century. William Robinson's *History and Antiquities of the Parish of Hackney*, of 1842-3, a blockbuster following up his slim *History and Antiquities of the Parish of Stoke Newington*, of 1820, is a fascinating ragbag of transcripts, lore and legend, newspaper cuttings, and accounts of parish institutions. Dr Benjamin Clarke, who wrote a series of newspaper articles under the pen-name 'FRCS', publishing them in 1894 as *Glimpses of Ancient Hackney and Stoke Newington*, offers much antiquarianism distilled from Robinson, and a very personal account of the transformation of the area from country settlement to London suburb. A facsimile edition, with illustrations and notes, was produced in 1986 by the Hackney Borough Council in association with the Hackney Society. David Mander's *Look Back, Look Forward* (1997), an account of Stoke Newington, and *Strength in the Tower* (1998), about Hackney, complete his very useful trilogy dealing with all three components of the modern London borough.

In 1995 Hackney was favoured with the long-awaited publication of volume X in the *Victoria County History of Middlesex*, by T.F.T. Baker, to range alongside Diane K. Bolton's account of Stoke Newington in volume VIII (1985). With these most new research about the area is henceforward likely to start.

One of the most useful texts setting Hackney in its context remains Millicent Rose's classic, *The East End of London* (1951); Alan Palmer's *The East End: Four Centuries of London Life* (1989) brings the wider picture more up to date. Contemporary inner city life is assessed from a wry Hackney perspective in Paul Harrison, *Inside the Inner City* (1983) and Patrick Wright, *A Journey through Ruins* (1991). Michael Hunter, *Victorian Villas of Hackney* (1981), Isobel Watson, *Gentlemen in the Building Line* (1989), Mary Cosh, *The New River* (2nd edition 1989), Ruth Paley, *Justice in 18th Century Hackney* (London Record Society vol. 28, 1991), David Solman, *Loddiges of Hackney: the largest hothouse in the world* (1995), and Jennifer Golden, *Hackney at War* (1995), all deal with special aspects of Hackney history. Geoff Taylor's *A Parish in Perspective* (2002), about South Hackney church and parish, *Sutton House* (2004), an English Heritage monograph by Belcher, Bond, Gray and Wittrick, and *De Beauvoir Town Millennium Scrapbook* (ed. Brian MacArthur, 1999) all enhance our appreciation of particular buildings and areas. There is also much excellent material on the built environment from the Hackney Society, especially *From Tower to Tower Block* (1979), focusing on buildings that survive, and Elizabeth Robinson's most valuable account of *Lost Hackney* (1989) as well as her *Twentieth Century Buildings in Hackney* (1999). Sutton Publishing have ranged widely across both Hackney and Stoke Newington in several volumes in the *Britain in Old Photographs* series, edited by David Mander and others.

Anyone seeking to keep abreast of new material about Hackney will however wish to keep an eye on *The Hackney Terrier* and *Hackney History*, the newsletter and annual journal of the Friends of Hackney Archives.

Introduction

The two names, Hackney and Stoke Newington, are commonly joined together. The two parishes, however, grew up with separate identities, Hackney in the forefront of suburban development, but Stoke Newington retaining its rural character for much longer until the railways allowed commuters to live there.

The two places were legally bound together only in the mid-nineteenth century, but this was shortlived, for in 1894 they went their own ways again, only to remarry in modern times within the new London Borough of Hackney.

Hackney has seen the most disruption since the tranquil days when the land was largely given over to market gardens and watercress beds. It has seen considerable social change as the wealthy, hemmed in by terraces, left their large houses to be redeveloped. In turn the terraced houses were let out in parts, and as fashion went west or into the leafier suburbs, so decay and dereliction set in – a tendency only reversed in the 1970s.

This book is an illustrated story of the changes which have taken place in both Hackney and Stoke Newington. I hope it will provoke curiosity about the architecture, institutions, place-names and social life and persuade residents to have an interest in their past that transforms into a stake in the future.

Isobel Watson, 1998.

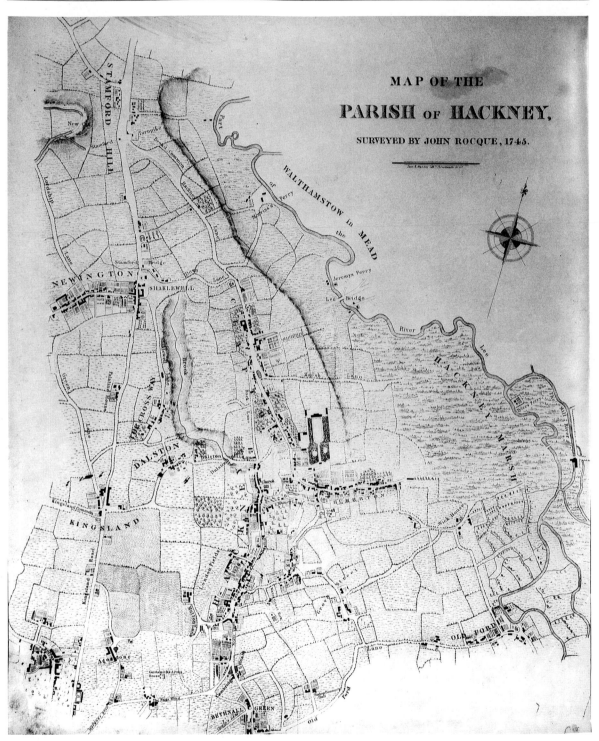

1. John Rocque's map of Hackney, 1745

2. *View of Hackney, showing Hackney village from the west in the mid-18th century.*

The Two Villages

A COLLECTION OF SETTLEMENTS

Stand at the foot of the old church tower, beside the small classical building that was Hackney's first town hall, and – with the railway bridge at your back – look north along the Narroway, that part of Mare Street which used to be called Church Street. The road curves gently up the hill, swings round to the right and then disappears towards Clapton Square. Just out of sight is the new church, a Georgian building which replaced the medieval structure whose tower, by which you stand, is the only remaining part. The plain, three-storey brick terraced buildings lining the street – still, despite successive widening, skirting it so tightly as to suggest the projecting timber buildings they disguise or replace – could belong to a small market town in almost any part of England. The atmosphere of the country village that Hackney once was has not been altogether lost. Indeed, the recent pedestrianisation of this part of Mare Street serves only to emphasise it.

The parishes of Hackney and Stoke Newington consisted, before development began in earnest in the early nineteenth century, of a dozen small settlements. The straggling village called Hackney was much the largest. Beginning at the Triangle, north of Cambridge Heath, it reached its highest and almost its northernmost point at Hackney old church. Here, the building was on elevated ground close to a highway junction: the road from Shoreditch to Stamford Hill was joined by that running east from Islington, and by the route through Homerton to the Lea marshes. The church also stood above the Hackney Brook, a stream whose line is approximately marked today by the line of Graham Road. Until a bridge was built across the Brook in 1790, Mare Street was forded just by its present junction with Amhurst Road.

Homerton was almost contiguous with Hackney village, 'Upper Homerton', the grander, western end beginning just beyond the Tudor mansion now known as Sutton House. Clapton (sometimes called Clopton) began just to the north, and straggled past its pond all the way to Newington Common. Shacklewell straddled the remnants of ancient common land around Shacklewell Green. Dalston (alternatively Durlston

3. (Above) Mare Street before the ford was bridged in 1790, from an etching by Morland.

4. Mare Street in 1805, showing the bridge, from a drawing by R. Schnebbelie.

or Dorleston) was originally a hamlet round similar waste manorial land at the 'elbow' in Dalston Lane. Kingsland was a small green where the road from Islington past Ball's Pond joined Ermine Street, the Roman road from London to Enfield. On the west side, south of Ball's Pond Road, stood a leper hospital and its associated chapel, dedicated to St Bartholomew. Founded in the late thirteenth century, it became in 1549 an outpost of the great medieval foundation of St Bartholomew at Smithfield. It was used as an out-ward until 1760, though the chapel survived and was used for worship until the site was cleared about 1846.

In the south of the parish lay Cambridge Heath, a settlement identified separately from that of Well Street, which began at its junction with Mare Street but spread eastwards, along the line of a tributary of the Hackney Brook to the probable site of the ancient well after which it was named. This lay north of the road, opposite where Holcroft Road and Lauriston Road now join it. To the south, Grove Street was a separate hamlet, the only one whose name has now wholly disappeared. It lay astride Lauriston Road, south of its

junction with Victoria Park Road, where, as in Shacklewell and Clapton, fragments of green by the roadside brighten the streetscape and link with the medieval past.

Stoke Newington has proper Greens, though they lie beyond its boundaries, Newington Green in Islington parish and Newington Common in Hackney. Newington Green was the point from which the settlement grew. It was the only hamlet in the area which was a roadside ribbon formation, but clustered around the village green and its well, and along the main road. Its oldest surviving domestic property, the brick terrace on the western side of the Green, at nos. 52 to 55, bears the date of 1658. It was only in the eighteenth century that the ancient thoroughfare along Church Street was extensively developed, and only from the later nineteenth, as the parish map on page 64 makes clear, that its density came to rival Hackney's.

5. The Lock Hospital and St Bartholomew's Chapel, the entrance to Ball's Pond Road and the Kingsland tollhouse. This watercolour bears a date of 1825.

6. *Stoke Newington from the north-west, from a Chatelain drawing of c1750.*

7. *St Mary's church from the New River, c1800.*

A HEALTHY PLACE

Hackney was the home of courtiers and rich merchants, who inhabited houses of the sixteenth century ranging from the comfortable to the opulent. It was a commonplace, in topographical guides from the early eighteenth century onwards, to remark that nearly a hundred gentlemen's carriages were kept there. (More carriages than Christians, according to one.)

Hackney, and Homerton, were known as places where ordinary Londoners might come to escape the stench of Westminster or the City in a hot summer, whether they took a house for the season or merely a coach for the afternoon. For Samuel and Elizabeth Pepys and their friends Hackney village was, with Islington, a favourite spot to which to go for a drive on a summer evening, ending at one of the taverns close by the old church, for 'cream and good cherries' and a game of shuffleboard. The traveller Celia Fiennes retired to be near her niece, who lived in Mare Street. She herself bought a house just to the south of the junction with Well Street, where she died in 1741.

By 1774, it was still fashionable to drive to Hackney to 'take the air': George III's Queen, Charlotte, chose such a drive for her first outing after a confinement, and a decade later still the actress Sarah Siddons stayed there to recover from an illness. Companies of City tradesmen would choose one of Hackney's hostelries for their annual celebration, particularly if their trade had a rural connotation – there are eighteenth-century accounts of the annual feast of the London florists, and the apothecaries' 'Herbalizing Feast'.

But a healthy reputation had to be safeguarded. In the 1750s, consciousness of the hardness of Hackney water drove summer visitors to more fashionable spas, and drew calls for the prosperous inhabitants to have water piped to them from Stoke Newington's New River. Instead, new waterworks were constructed on the Lea, and a reservoir was built north of Clapton Pond.

Its reputation made Hackney the natural choice when, in 1768, a physician set up an establishment, in the Ivy House, Mare Street (at its present junction with Richmond Road) for the sole purpose of offering inoculation against smallpox. This so alarmed the inhabitants, however, that (despite the doctor's assertion that his neighbours were as likely to catch smallpox from association with his

8. Homerton High Street, looking north from Ponsford Street: a watercolour, c.1840

patients as by looking through a telescope from Hampstead) the premises were discreetly closed.

As in a number of healthy and respectable suburbs around inner London, Hackney was a popular choice in which to found private schools. To the Restoration dramatists 'Hackney School' housed the daughters of wealthy citizens of London, whom Pepys admired at church. Pupils were too integrated into village life for the taste of one fastidious young man – Dudley Ryder, later Attorney General – who, in his diary, noted that at a dance he attended in 1715 he had 'too much company of the schoolgirls'. In the eighteenth century 'Hackney School' was synonymous with Dr Newcome's Academy for 'young noblemen and gentlemen'.

9. The King's Head, 1853, by T.C. Dibdin. This building, which was demolished in 1879, dated from the 16th century. It stood on the east side of Mare Street opposite the present junction with Graham Road.

10. A City victuallers' feast in 1846, held as fund-raising for the Victuallers' School, then at Lambeth. The site appears to be the Mermaid gardens, looking south-west. Hackney had been a resort for this type of gathering for more than a century, but railway and housing development would soon send them further afield. The aquatint is by G. Hunt, after E. F. Lambert.

ROOM FOR DISSENT

Many combined a permanent residence in the villages with a business in the City. The Ryders, for example, ran a draper's business in Cheapside in the early part of the eighteenth century, but also maintained a home in what is now Urswick Road. As Dissenters they, like the Fiennes connections, will have been attracted to the place by its combination of nearness to London with a tradition of toleration for those who refused to accept the teachings of the established church. From the seventeenth century, dissenting sects and their meeting houses flourished and multiplied in both Hackney and Stoke Newington, where there was a well-known college for non-conformist ministers which counted Daniel Defoe amongst its students. At the same time there was also an increasing number of wealthy Jewish settlers of Spanish or Portuguese descent who made their homes in these parishes.

BUILDING THE PARISH CHURCHES

A church dedicated to St Augustine, the 'apostle to the English', was in existence at Hackney by the close of the thirteenth century. Perhaps some of its fabric survives in Hackney's oldest building, the church tower, which is all that is left of the St Augustine's that was rebuilt in the early sixteenth century. The change of local saint from St Augustine to St John took place some time after this, and is usually attributed to the presence in the parish of substantial landholdings of the Order of St John of Jerusalem, based in Clerkenwell, who acquired the property of the Knights Templar when that Order was suppressed. The Templars also gave their name to Temple Mills, and to an ancient house that stood beyond the north end of Mare Street, opposite the junction with Clarence Road (or 'Back lane', as it was then called).

The old church of St Augustine housed opulent monuments to the medieval courtiers, landowners and merchants who had made Hackney their home. Some of these monuments were transferred in the 1790s to the vast new church of St John-at-Hackney. They include that of Christopher Urswick, the powerful adviser to Henry VII, who was, as

11. St Augustine's church, partly demolished, as it looked in 1798. A watercolour by John Varley.

12. *Hackney churchyard about 1830, a watercolour by George Hawkins. On the right is the Old Town Hall. The range of buildings on the south side of the churchyard includes the home of the surveyor M. A. Gliddon (1819-1869), one of Hackney's early historians.*

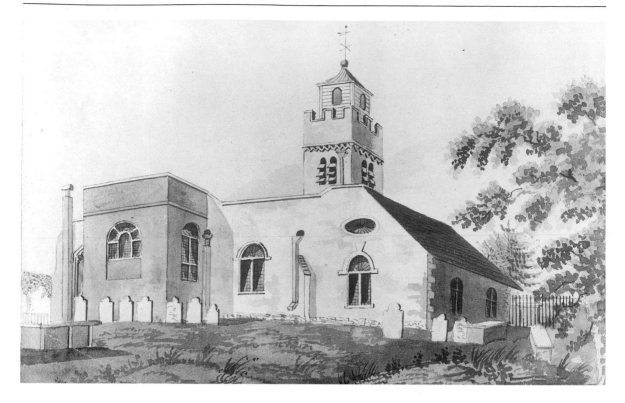

13. *St Mary's old church, Stoke Newington, from the south west. A watercolour, c1800.*

14. *St Mary's Rectory, Stoke Newington, demolished in 1855 to make way for the new church. A watercolour of 1911.*

rector, also responsible for rebuilding the old church in 1509. Though heavily repaired in 1720, by the middle of the eighteenth century the old church had become too cramped for the ever-growing population. The churchyard also had to be closed for new interments in the 1760s, when an extension was made. By this time the church's association with St Augustine had faded, and it had come to be known as St John-at-Hackney. A new church was mooted in 1756, and again in the 1770s. The move came to nothing at that time, it was said, because of 'the distressed situation of publick Affairs', in other words the difficulty of raising money. By the 1780s, it was found that the thousand or so houses in the parish at mid-century had increased since then by half as many again. It was estimated that a new church would need to seat 3,000, a number calculated on the optimistic assumption that the seating capacity of the medieval building accounted for numerous families deserting their mother church, and flocking to the charismatic preaching at the dissenters' meeting houses.

In the face of much local dissension, an Act of Parliament was obtained in 1790, and an architect, William Blackburn, appointed. Within months he was dead, and replaced by a much younger man, James Spiller, who produced new plans which went into production in 1792. After five years, and more than one attempt at securing adequate finance, the church was consecrated in July 1797, though it was not until 1812 that the money could be raised to add the porches and Spiller's unique tower. In the meantime, although the old church had been knocked down in 1798 (some of its fabric going to build the bridge fording the Hackney Brook the following year), the tower had been kept to house the peal of bells, the new tower not being trusted to bear their weight. Here they stayed until 1854, when the new structure was underpinned. By this time the populace had begun to regret the disappearance of the remainder of the ancient building.

They may have envied the parishioners of Stoke Newington, who succeeded in holding on to their old building. St Mary's, associated from the fourteenth century with the dean and chapter of St Paul's, was rebuilt in 1563. Its monuments include that of Elizabeth, wife of Thomas Sutton, founder of Charterhouse. Throughout the eighteenth century the church had to be restored and enlarged, and despite repair and renewal, the drainage was

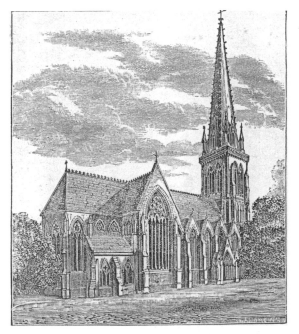

15. St Mary's new church, Stoke Newington, from the south-east. From a drawing by W. Andrews. The spire was added in 1890.

so bad that in 1827 coffins were found floating beneath the church floor. By the early 1850s its small size was no longer tolerable, even though extra accommodation had been provided for the parish with the building of St Matthias.

There was local controversy as to whether rebuilding was necessary, the economy-minded Low Church members of the congregation joining to oppose it along with the High Church members of rival St Matthias; but in 1853 George Gilbert Scott was commissioned to build a new St Mary's to accommodate twice the number that could be comfortable in the old. But the parishioners of Stoke Newington wisely kept the old church and it remained in regular use. At the end of the nineteenth century its appeal was described as being that of 'an old fashioned service to old fashioned worshippers'. When new St Mary's was damaged by bombing in the Second World War, the principal parish services were held once again in the old church.

Farms and Gardens

FOOD FOR LONDON

Before systematic development began, both Hackney and Stoke Newington depended economically almost entirely on agriculture and market gardening. So near the City of London, the produce of the fertile fields fed the population's appetites. The traveller leaving Shoreditch and riding towards Kingsland would find, beyond the built-up area, that the road was bordered by meadows, until, on reaching Balmes House (which stood near the present line of Downham Road) hayfields could be seen stretching westwards towards Canonbury. Meadows also surrounded Newington Green. Such land between Kingsland and Stamford Hill as was not used for grazing sheep, or dairy and beef cattle, was parkland attached to the homes of the wealthy.

Turning east where the road joined Ball's Pond Road, beside a substantial nursery, the lane through Dalston would pass other nursery grounds, until in Hackney village the scene would reveal a patchwork of market gardens. They lay on either side of the Hackney Brook stretching all the way past Homerton, behind the straggling line of Mare Street, and covered most of the area along the boundary with Bethnal Green parish where Victoria Park was later formed.

Near Balmes were watercress beds: we know this because of a poignant report of the drowning of a small boy while his mother was gathering cress in 1759. There were other watercress fields at Pond Lane (Millfields Road). But the most extensive beds were those along the north side of Morning Lane, irrigated originally by the Hackney Brook but from the 1840s by well-water, after it became clear that the brook was polluted by sewage. Local lore had it that these were the first systematically farmed watercress beds in the country. They survived the building of the railway, until Chalgrove Road was built in 1875.

The sandy soil was well-suited to agriculture. In 1799, a field in the recently laid-out Cassland Road was chosen for trials for a newly-invented type of horse plough, made at forges in Covent Garden and specially designed so that the plough could be drawn by one horse instead of four.

The most extensive grazing ground was in the marshes, which, like most other common land in Hackney, was Lammas land. By customary law, after Lammas Day (1st August according to the

16. Barn and cottages at Hackney Wick, c1840.

17. A Stoke Newington granary, shown later as a Congregational chapel. By T. H. Shepherd, c1844.

old calendar, and 12th August from 1752 onwards) it was expected that the landowners would have cleared away their crops, and all the tenants of the manor were permitted to turn their beasts on to the land for the winter. Most of the extent of Hackney Downs, the marsh land, Well Street Common and the Mill Fields were used for arable crops, often corn and barley, until the mid-nineteenth century. The crops would be taken to the mills in the Lea Valley for grinding.

An extraordinary incident in 1837 could be seen as symbolising the end of rural Hackney. It had been a bad summer, and by twelfth August much of the crop was still uncut. Word spread that not only were the local people entitled to put their animals on to the Common, but that they also owned whatever might still be growing there. According to the press, thousands of people thronged to the Downs, reaping till past midnight despite the protestations of the farmer. The manorial customs and authority which still governed the land had ceased to have any real meaning to the local population. But agricultural use persisted to a surprisingly late date. The owners of the Lammas land of Well Street Common were

18. A farm cottage south of Well Street, near Shore Road, a watercolour by Charles Bigot c1845. Cottages in this neighbourhood had the evocative name of Water Gruel Row.

19. Watercress beds between Morning Lane and the North London railway: a watercolour of 1853 by T. C. Dibdin. A coal train is travelling east along the viaduct.

attempting to grow arable crops there as late as the 1850s, and when grazing use followed, the beasts found themselves in competition with the local cricketers.

THE LODDIGES NURSERY

The most famous of several Hackney nurseries lay east of Mare Street. The business had been founded about 1760, near London Lane, by one German, John Busch, and taken over by another, Conrad Loddiges, when Busch went to Russia to design landscaped gardens in the 'English style' for Catherine the Great. Loddiges had first come to Hackney as gardener to Dr John Silvester (who had a large house near the old path to the church which is now named after him). Eventually he held about fifteen acres of land belonging to St Thomas's Hospital, where Loddiges and Darnley Roads now meet. The Loddiges family collected exotic plants from all corners of the world, and developed a special system of steam central heating to nurture a wide variety of hothouse specimens, including palms and orchids. There were also temperate houses for ferns and camellias, and a huge circular bed containing all the known varieties of rose. The business's catalogue, first issued in 1777, was printed in Latin, English and German; its distinction was maintained with the publication, in 1817, of the first issue of *The Botanical Cabinet*, which became famous for its superb colour plates.

The Loddiges nursery introduced many new species to British gardens; Conrad Loddiges supplied the Duke of Devonshire's garden at Chatsworth as his predecessor Busch had supplied the royal garden at Kew. When, in 1860, the business finally closed, giving way to streets of small terraced houses, the enormous trees from the 40 foot palm house were taken in slow, dignified procession all the way to their new home at the Crystal Palace.

20. Title page from The Botanical Cabinet, published in 1826.

21. One of the plates, by George Cooke, from The Botanical Cabinet.

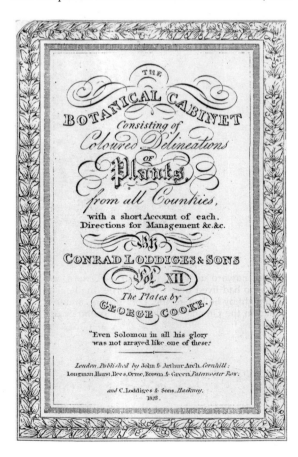

22. The Black and White House, a lithograph by Dean and Munday of the early 1840s.

The Great Houses

BROOKE HOUSE AND OTHERS

Hackney village contained several substantial town houses of the sixteenth century. The Black and White House, immediately beside the churchyard to the south of St Augustine's tower, was the home of Sir Thomas Vyner, a City magnate of the seventeenth century. Legend associates the house with James I's daughter, the Queen of Bohemia – hence Bohemia Place. Evidence for this is no better, however, than for the legend which associates Elizabeth I with Stoke Newington. (The supposed connection of Edward IV's mistress, Jane Shore, with Shore Place in South Hackney is pure invention.)

Better authenticated is the origin of the King's Place, later Brooke House, which stood at the junction of Lower Clapton Road and Brooke Road. It dated probably from the late fifteenth century, and passed in the 1530s from Henry Percy, Earl of Northumberland (whose brief association with Hackney has spawned over the years a surprising number of commemoratively named villas, streets and pubs) via Thomas Cromwell to Henry VIII, who visited the house on several occasions. It was here Henry met, and was reconciled with, his daughter, Mary, in 1536; his Lord Chancellor used the house as a refuge from the plague raging in London in 1544. After the death of Edward de Vere, 17th Earl of Oxford, in 1604, who had lived here with his wife, the house was bought by Fulke Greville, Lord Brooke, and remained in the Greville family for two centuries. It underwent further rebuilding in the mid-seventeenth century, and later acquired eighteenth-century Gothic features as well as a classical east front. It became common for Hackney houses, too large to be sustained once fashion had taken their wealthy owners elsewhere, to be turned over for institutional use, and Brooke House was typical. It was used as a private lunatic asylum from 1758 until its sad end from bomb damage.

By the time that John Evelyn and, later, Samuel Pepys visited Brooke House, its Tudor architecture had become distinctly unfashionable. Pepys did not care for the house, and Evelyn found it 'a despicable building'. But they had been

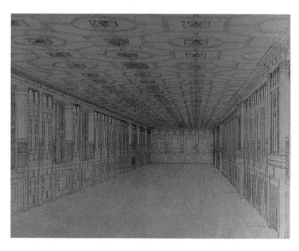

23. *Brooke House from the south-east, in 1750.*
By Chatelain.

24. *The Long Gallery in Brooke House, in 1844.*
By G. Toussaint.

25. *The east front of Brooke House in 1844.*
By G. Toussaint.

26. *Balmes House, a view published by Robinson in his 'History and Antiquities of Hackney', 1842. The house is accurately based on contemporary drawings by Toussaint, but a fanciful perspective of St Leonard's Shoreditch is conjured up alongside the windmill of the former white lead factory on the Islington side of what is now Southgate Road.*

27. *Robinson also presents this view of Balmes 'from an old print', elsewhere dated to 1707. The Kingsland Road is on the top right of the engraving, and the avenue of trees to the east of the house corresponds with the later line of Mortimer Road at its southern end.*

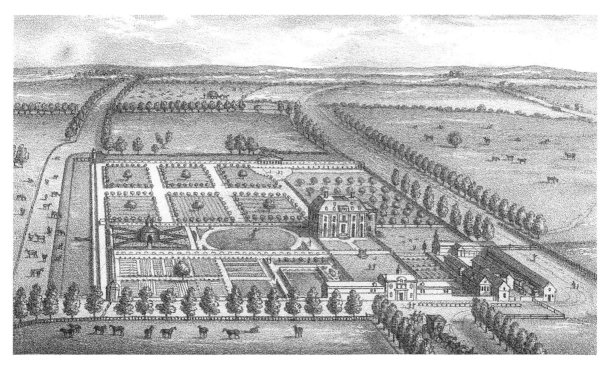

brought here by the gardens, which Pepys found 'excellent'. There was a great variety of exotic plants, and 'several Labarinths and a pretty aviary'. Here he first saw oranges growing, and was so intrigued that he stole one (it was a disappointment, being 'just as other little green small oranges are').

Some idea of the formal gardens at Brooke House may be gained from illustration 27, which shows the garden layout at Balmes House, also visited by Pepys in its days as the residence of Sir George Whitmore, who built the house. It was originally moated. The gardens included lawns, parterres, orchards and what may have been another 'labarinth', as well as the ornamental canal which replaced the moat. The house itself (see also illustration 26) was a very curious example of a hybrid between classical and European vernacular building styles.

Equally curious is another house of the sixteenth century, which had no name that has survived it, but was sketched by the antiquary William Stukeley. This house stood in South Hackney, on the east side of the path from Bow to Well Street, approxi-

mately where Penshurst and Lauriston Roads now meet, and belonged to Henry Norris, a City merchant and magistrate. Stukeley has noted on his sketch 'This is a model of our antient way of building'.

The house also had an extraordinary garden, more productive than ornamental. An inventory shows the garden itself, which seems to have consisted, like much of the Balmes estate, of formal tree-lined walks, as containing vines, nectarines and mulberries, pear and Kentish cherry trees, walnut, quince and apple trees of different varieties, and numerous plum trees. There were strawberry, raspberry and asparagus beds, and gooseberry and currant bushes. Illustration 29 shows the whole estate, including the garden, on its inheritance by Henry Handley Norris in 1803.

The mid eighteenth century fashion for landscaping is seen most starkly in the layout shown on John Rocque's 1745 map (illustration 1) for the grounds of Hackney House. Rocque's map shows intriguing differences from the layout projected in the plan shown on page 31. The house, which

28. The Norris house, South Hackney, when occupied by Robert Ainsworth in 1725. By William Stukeley.

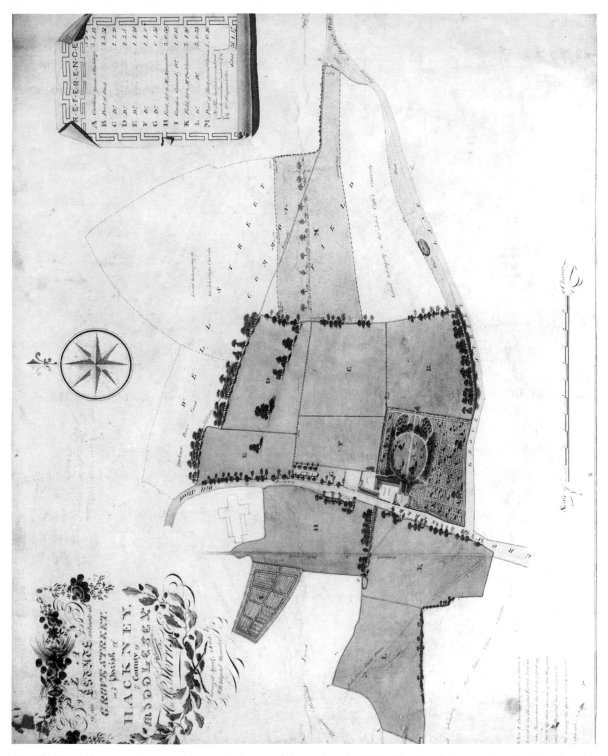

29. *The Norris house and estate, showing the layout of the gardens in 1803. The site of the new church of St John of Jerusalem has been added in the 1840s.*

30. *Hackney House, before extension in the 1780s. From a lithograph by Richard Ward.*

stood approximately where Median Road now meets Glenarm Road, with an entrance drive along the line of Tresham Avenue, was built about 1730 for Stamp Brooksbank, a financier of local descent who became Governor of the Bank of England. The design is associated with the influential Palladian, Colen Campbell, famous for the much grander Wanstead House. Something of the scale and appearance of Hackney House, can be understood today from Campbell's surviving Stourhead, although the landscaping designed for Brooksbank appears to have been rather more formal. The associated estate was vast, stretching as far south as Homerton Row in the south and Millfields Road in the north, and to the east all the way to the Lea cut.

In 1786 Hackney House was acquired for Hackney New College, established to train ministers in the Calvinist tradition, and wings were added to west and east, one of them by the same William Blackburn who later nearly became the architect of St John's parish church. But the College, despite its influence, was short-lived, and the house was demolished ten years later, its grounds being broken up for a number of villas. The main Clapton road was already dotted with villas, including a group

to which the name of the Five Houses became attached, inhabited by the City merchants and manufacturers who were increasingly making Hackney their country retreat.

SUTTON HOUSE

Of other grand houses, such as those at the north western end of Homerton High Street, little is known and nothing remains. Here around the beginning of the seventeenth century Lord Zouche had a magnificent garden under the supervision of Matthias de l'Obel, after whom the lobelia is named, but its location remains in doubt. It is exceptional good fortune that a substantial merchant's house does survive, and has recently undergone the most thorough structural and documentary investigation. This is, of course, the house at the west end of Homerton now known as Sutton House. Though the house, built in 1535, was attributed earlier this century to Sir Thomas Sutton, founder of Charterhouse School and hospital, Sutton was no more than the neighbouring landowner. The originator of the house was Sir Ralph Sadleir, a prominent courtier and later Henry VIII's ambassador to Scotland. He referred to it as 'the bryk place', its solidity through brick

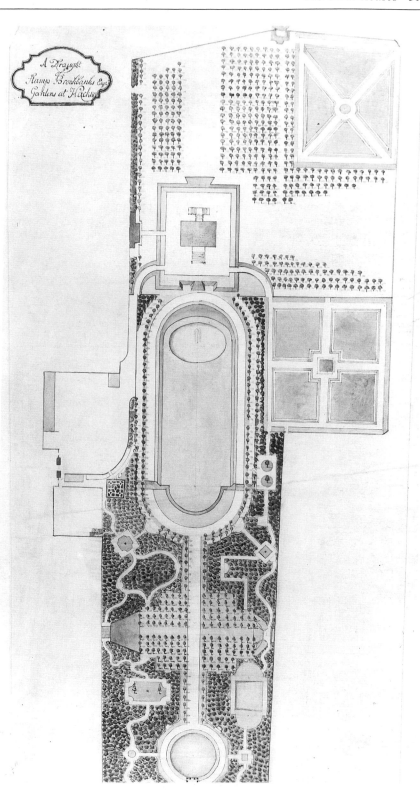

A Draught
Hamp: Brookbanks Esq.
Gardens at Hackny

31. A design for the gardens
of Hackney House, executed
(probably with variations
from this plan) before 1745.

construction comparing favourably with the King's own possession, later known as Brooke House. 'The brick place' was the Sadleir family home until 1550, when they moved to Standon in Hertfordshire. The house passed from the court to the City, Sadleir's successor being John Machell, whose death in 1558 frustrated his accession to the mayoralty. By 1650 it had followed the path of so many large Hackney houses, then and later, by being turned over, not for the first time, for use as a school. Indeed the house was divided into two halves by the mid eighteenth century, the western part another school. In 1890 it was reunified by the rector, Lord Wenlock, who transformed it into the St John's Church Institute, a social centre for young men of the district. Alterations from this period include the basement chapel, and the hall now called Wenlock Barn, which forms part of the charming courtyard and encloses the Tudor 'H'. In 1938 the National Trust acquired the house, after a public appeal led by George Lansbury and supported by the Society for the Protection of Ancient Buildings and the London County Council's Survey Committee. In 1953 the Trust gave 'the old

house on the corner' the name of Sutton House, though more recent research has established that all Sutton did was to leave his lands to the west (and his house known as 'the tan house', which was demolished in the early nineteenth century in connection with the development of Sutton Place) as part of his endowment of Charterhouse on his death in 1605.

Used for some forty years as offices, by the 1980s the house was empty and vandalised; part of its Tudor panelling had been stolen, but later recovered. A scheme to divide it up into residential flats was thwarted by local residents, and in 1989 the Trust established a local committee of management to oversee its restoration for educational and other community uses.

32. Sutton House, when in use as St John's Church Institute, 1900.

STOKE NEWINGTON HOUSES

Stoke Newington had, as well as the manor house on the site of what became Church Row, its own grand houses, in extensive grounds on the north side of Church Street. Fleetwood House, built in the 1630s, altered and enlarged throughout the eighteenth century and replaced in 1872 by Fleetwood Street, was named after its second owner, one of Cromwell's generals. Its easterly neighbour, Abney House, was begun in the last years of the 1690s by Thomas Gunston, and passed on his death in 1700 to his sister, who had married an Abney. It was known by various names, including that of 'Lady Abney's House', and then, in the early nineteenth century, as the 'Manor House'. The hymn writer, Isaac Watts, then living at Fleetwood House, designed wall paintings for the interior panelling. He lived here with his patrons, the Abneys, describing the house in verse as 'solid and square', with an air 'manly and plain. Such was the builder's soul'. T.H. Shepherd was commissioned to paint the house's elegant interiors before its demolition in 1843; as well as recording the detail of the rooms, he produced conjectural pictures of Dr Watts in his study and in the garden.

All that remains of the house are the fine wrought iron gates, which form the Church Street entrance to the cemetary which now occupies its grounds.

Abney Park Cemetery, Hackney's equivalent of Highgate, Kensal Green and Nunhead, was laid out from its beginnings in 1839 to perpetuate Stoke Newington's tradition of religious tolerance, while providing an alternative to the City's overburdened Bunhill Fields as a burial ground for non-Anglicans. The project was masterminded by George Collison, son of the founder of the evangelical Theological Seminary in Well Street, and the grounds laid out by Loddiges. Among the eminent bones interred there are those of Samuel Morley, the educational philanthropist, Andrew Reed, founder of the London Orphan Asylum, William and Catherine Booth, founders of the Salvation Army; and James Braidwood, father of modern firefighting.

Many of the grand houses saw out their days as institutions – more rarely as family houses – before falling prey to the pressures of housing development. Less happy was the fate of Hackney's Shore House, in Shore Road, and the so-called Templars' House, at the north-east tip of Mare Street, so named supposedly through association with the Knights Templar. In the hands of absent landowners they gradually deteriorated, by the eighteenth century being used as rooming-houses (the Templars' also as a tavern), and they were ultimately demolished because of their ruinous condition.

33. Fleetwood House, 1843, by T.H. Shepherd.

34. *Abney House, c1843, by T.H. Shepherd*

35. *The entrance to Abney Park cemetery, c1845.*

36. *The manor house, Shacklewell Lane. It stood north-west of Shacklewell Lane, near the present Seal and Perch Streets. It was demolished in the mid eighteenth century.*

The Lords of the Manor

THE TYSSENS

Hackney was divided into several ancient manors, the most important of which were those called Lordshold and Kingshold. The extensive manor of Lordshold, which stretched across from Shacklewell to Homerton and Grove Street (Lauriston Road) was confiscated from the Wentworth family during the Commonwealth, and sold to one William Hobson. Hobson also bought Kingshold, which had descended from the Knights Templar via the Order of St John of Jerusalem, and included land in South Hackney and Hackney Wick. These manors were subsequently transferred to Sir Thomas Cooke, the owner of a house in extensive grounds at the north-west end of Homerton High Street.

In 1697, both manors were bought by Francis Tyssen, a merchant of Dutch descent, who had settled a few years earlier on an estate bought from the Rowe family, formerly seen as Hackney's leading inhabitants, whose descendants ultimately declined into pauperdom. The Tyssen estate, the most extensive in Hackney, stretched from Kingsland Road in the west to the Upper and Lower Clapton Roads in the east, and from Dalston village northwards as far as Stamford Hill.

The Tyssen home at Shacklewell Green, on Shacklewell Lane, became known as the Manor House. This was a house of the later part of the seventeenth century, replacing an older house in whose grounds it stood. The latter had belonged to the Herons, connected by marriage with Sir Thomas More, and associated with the rebuilding of St Augustine's Church. Later, in Mare Street's Narroway, the name of 'Manor House' became attached to a double-fronted house built in the 1840s for the Tyssen who acted as manor steward, and which, much altered, still stands.

The seventeenth century had seen City traders settling in Hackney in increasing numbers, and the wealthier and titled residents beginning to depart. The end of the century, and the sale of the Rowe estate, can perhaps be seen as marking the end of

37. (Above) A house in Well Street, formerly the property of the Order of St John, which by the end of the eighteenth century was inhabited by chimney sweeps. It stood opposite the junction with Cassland Road.

38. Sir Thomas Rowe. A copy of an oil portrait.

Hackney's tenuous claim to association with royalty and the court, and its becoming more firmly the resort of a comfortable *haute bourgeoisie*. Not that the early Tyssens did not have grandiose and courtly pretensions. Francis Tyssen's funeral procession in 1717, with its sixty horsemen, thirty-six coaches and six, and four king's trumpeters among many others, took three hours of procession from Goldsmiths' Hall to Hackney church. Its extravagance drew a public rebuke from the Earl Marshal as being wholly inappropriate to the deceased's social standing, as a mere citizen and commoner.

Francis John Tyssen, who died in 1781, was probably the last Lord of the Manor to live in Hackney. By 1892, when William Amhurst Tyssen-Amherst was created the first Baron Amherst of Hackney, the family had long spent most of their time on their Norfolk estates. It is to John Robert Daniel-Tyssen, the first baron's uncle, who acted as manor steward, that modern Hackney owes most. His collection of books and documents, formerly known as the Tyssen Library, forms the nucleus of the borough's historical archive.

STOKE NEWINGTON MANORS

Most of the manor of Stoke Newington belonged to the cathedral of St Paul's. The exception was an erratically shaped area, centreing on the present-day Milton and Spenser Groves and Walford Road which, through an ancient quirk of landowner-ship, formed (until 1900) part, not of Stoke Newington, but of the parish of South Hornsey. The original Stoke Newington manor house stood close to the church. The status of lord of the manor, with attendant rights to make money from land transfers, was let out to individuals, passing eventually to the Abneys.

In both Hackney and Stoke Newington there would be regular sessions of the manorial court, usually held at a convenient hostelry, at which land sales would be confirmed, heirs admitted to tenure of the estates of those who had died, and any dispute about interference with common land considered.

As the nineteenth century progressed the power of the lords of the manor gradually waned. Interference with common land look place – such as that by William Rhodes, building on part of London Fields – with the lord of the manor acting to protect the common interest. Copyhold land, which originally could not be leased for long enough to make building worthwhile without a substantial fee being payable, was enfranchised without difficulty, for cash. Though their control over privately held land swiftly diminished, the Tyssens were, as will be seen, able to secure substantial sums for buying out their residual rights in the Hackney commons.

39. The rebuilt Manor House at Shacklewell, which replaced that shown in illustration 36 in the latter half of the eighteenth century. It was demolished about 1880.

40. Gillray's view of a Hackney meeting to protest at the terms of the Convention of Cintra, 1808. Under this treaty Wellington permitted the French army occupying Portugal to withdraw.

Village Pastimes

THE VILLAGE INNS

At the beginning of the eighteenth century between fifty and sixty justices' licences, for inns, taverns and alehouses would be granted each year. Most of these were for unremarkable local or roadside pubs, but a few had pretensions. These must have included the coffee houses which flourished briefly in the latter half of the century, one in Church Street (founded by Sir John Silvester), another, briefly, in Shacklewell.

Pre-eminent amongst all the Hackney hostelries was the Mermaid, scene of political and parish meetings, as well as of any gathering where large numbers were expected. Home in the early nineteenth century to the 'Hackney Assembly', where fashionable Hackney would go to see and be seen, the Mermaid's extensive pleasure grounds, on the west side of Mare Street north of the Hackney Brook, were also used, from 1811, for several spectacular ascents by the professional balloonist,

James Sadler, and his clients. Rebuilt as the 'Manor Rooms', named by association with the adjacent house built by the Tyssens, here were held innumerable popular entertainments. Here also 800 members of literary- and scientific-minded Hackney established in 1848 an Institution, for debating artistic, philosophical and scientific subjects and for the display of curiosities from their private collections. Towards the end of the nineteenth century the pleasure garden was covered over, briefly becoming a skating rink in the 1870s, before the area was developed for housing. But room was left for the short-lived Manor Cinema to be established in Kenmure Road about 1912.

On the east side of the street the King's Head and, close to the churchyard, the Old Mermaid, were basic, local pubs. The Old Mermaid tended to have a seedy clientele, from the strolling players who gave great offence to upright parishioners in the 1760s, to characters nicknamed 'the human hog' and 'the Hackney bulldog' in the 1840s. The landlord of the King's Head, according to legend, missed a trick on the restoration of the monarchy;

41. *An advertisement for entertainment at the Mermaid in Hackney, in c1822.*

42. *(Right) A grand fete and fireworks display at the Mermaid in 1822.*

43. Fashionable Hackney at the Hackney Assembly Rooms at the Mermaid, as seen by Rowlandson, 1812.

44. Sadler's balloon at the Mermaid gardens, 1811.

during the Commonwealth the pub had been called the Cromwell's Head, and he wasn't quick enough to move with the times to change the name and save himself from the pillory.

The Rose and Crown and the Falcon were amongst the most long-standing of numerous public houses in Stoke Newington Church Street. On the High Street, the Three Crowns was typical of the coaching inns, which also included the White Hart at Clapton (rebuilt after a fire in 1831), and the Flying Horse in Mare Street, opposite Well Street. The White Swan, now just the Swan, at Upper Clapton, as well as serving the coaching trade and its passengers, was, like Hackney's Mermaid, the scene for voting at local and national elections.

Other publicans made their livelihood from attracting people from the City and other built up areas. For example, the tea gardens of the Three Colts, where today Lauriston Road meets Gore Road, were an easy afternoon's stroll north-east from Bethnal Green across Bishop Bonner's Fields.

45. *The Falcon Inn, Stoke Newington Church Street, in 1844, by T. H. Shepherd. It was rebuilt in 1854, and stood on the site of 151 Church Street until the early 1930s.*

46. *The Three Crowns, on the corner of Stoke Newington's Church Street and High Street, by T. H. Shepherd, 1843. A pub on this site was so called between 1683 and 1989. Legend has it that the name alluded to James I, passing this way on his first journey to London; though in the seventeenth century the pub seems to have had other names, including the Flower de Luce. The present building, of 1898, remains in use as a bar.*

47. *The Old Flying Horse, a coaching inn on the west side of Mare Street, south of its junction with Well Street.*

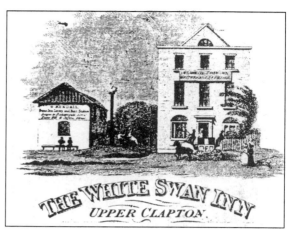

48. (Left) The Rose and Crown, Stoke Newington Church Street, 1843. Watercolour by T.H. Shepherd. This building, of 1815, replaced a 200-year-old timber-framed building. Its modern successor was moved from the east to the west side of Albion Road.

49. (Below) The Swan Inn on Clapton Common, c1830.

50. (Bottom) The Cat and Mutton, London Fields, drawing by Bigot in 1811.

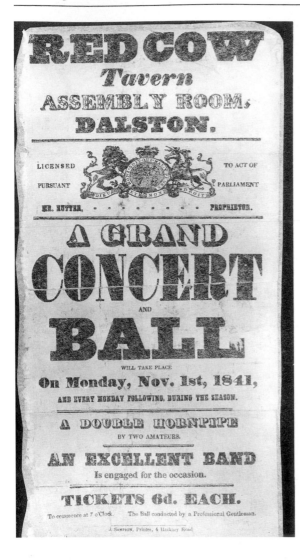

51. (Left) Poster for an event at the Red Cow, Dalston, in 1841.

52. (Above) The Three Colts Tavern, c1840.

or just rested, to return for tea, songs from the bridegroom's father and a supper about nine o'clock. They ordered their carriages for ten, leaving the newlyweds to honeymoon in Hackney.

On the northern fringes of Hackney was the grand Hornsey Wood Tavern, so successful that it was extensively enlarged. Amongst its attractions was angling in an artificial lake, now part of Finsbury Park. The New River, constructed under the authority of Parliament first given in 1605, to bring fresh water to north London from springs in Hertfordshire, was a boon to anglers from the beginning. They could also seek refreshments at the Eel Pie House, on a loop of the New River at Highbury. But the fishing here was unlikely to rival the Horse and Groom, Jolly Anglers and White House on the Lea, which offered perch, roach, dace, chub, gudgeon, barbel, carp and eels.

Towards the Lea, there were also other sporting attractions. In the late 1720s a hostelry in the Marsh was known as the Rubbing House, suggesting an association with horse-racing, which is known to have taken place thereabouts a decade later. At Marsh Gate, the name of the Greyhound indicates the sport which was on offer.

THE VILLAGE SPORTS

The publicans often sponsored sporting events. The Rosemary Branch tavern (a resort for Islington, Finsbury and Hoxton as well as Hackney) had considerable ground where pony-racing was held. Open spaces, including Hackney Downs and Hackney Marshes, were also the scene of horse-racing – in 1737 the novelty on the Marshes was that the horses would swim rather than run.

At the Cat and Mutton on London Fields, for a

Or a stroll north might end at the Cat and Mutton, on London Fields, which was in being (under its original name of the Shoulder of Mutton) by 1722. The name came from the shape of the fields themselves, sometimes called Shoulder of Mutton Fields. The Red Cow, Dalston's answer to the Mermaid, lasted until Wayland Avenue was built over its pleasure gardens from 1867. The George at Clapton was described in the 1720s as 'in the Country'.

The King's Arms at Upper Clapton prided itself on its 'ordinary', or table d'hôte. The celebration of a wedding joining two Huguenot families from Spitalfields in the 1780s took place at the Two Black Boys in Well Street, a hostelry first licensed in 1727. After a lavish 'dinner' in the middle of the day, the company went driving or walking,

53. *Eel Pie House and Sluice House on the New River at Highbury, c1845.*

54. *Hornsey Wood Tavern, c1845, whose grounds now form part of Finsbury Park. A fashionable resort, especially for angling, this tavern was rebuilt on the site of an old roadside inn. This has been the meeting place for the manorial court of Brownswood Manor.*

time, the weekly attraction offered was an entertainment whereby the tail of a pig was greased, and each contestant – unsuccessfully – attempted to swing the animal round his head. Another, probably short-lived, attraction in the marshes was bull-baiting. The bull was attacked by a dozen dogs and, as the final attraction, set loose amongst the crowd. Probably the problem of keeping order as much as growing public distaste accounts for the disappearance of this 'sport' after the 1790s.

An alternative, should animal torture fail to amuse, was prize-fighting. Some very grisly contests took place, both as a set-piece rival attraction to the bull-baiting, and as a regular attraction in the pubs nearer London. Casual grudge matches took place on London Fields. By the mid-nineteenth century fighting was provided for in a more ordered fashion, in the ring specially set up by John Baum at the White Lion, Hackney Wick. Baum also maintained an athletics track where regular events were held. In 1863 there was

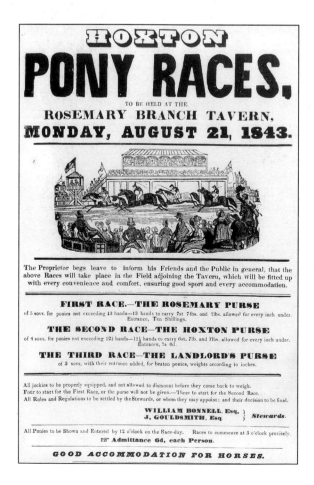

55. *Hoxton Pony Races, 1843*

56. *Rowlandson's view of a women's cricket match Hampshire vs Surrey - near Kingsland in 1811*

57. *Boxing at the White Lion, Hackney Wick, 1862. The impresario at this time, John Baum, moved on to become the last manager of the Cremorne Gardens at Chelsea.*

an all-comers challenge by the American Indian runner, Deerfoot. Deerfoot lost the contest, but Baum, who was also a property developer, rather pleasingly named a row of cottages in his honour.

The only athletics event in which it seems to have been thought appropriate for women to participate was also a popular custom at village festivals throughout England: a smock race. In eighteenth-century Hackney a holiday event at the Rosemary Branch or on the marshes might include a race between women for the prize of a fine linen smock. These spectacles, which had about them an air of social condescension, seem to have fallen out of favour as nineteenth-century notions of propriety took hold.

When in 1811 Rowlandson (illustration 56) notes what is evidently very much out of the ordinary, a women's cricket match at Ball's Pond, near Kingsland, between representatives of Hampshire and Surrey, the flavour of his commentary is scarcely approving, and there is an innuendo, as with the smock races, that the event was organised for the edification of gentlemen sponsors.

Men's cricket was, naturally, another matter. Cricketfield Road marks the site of a long-standing pitch. London Fields saw the beginning of club cricket in Hackney, clubs being established by 1802. London Fields played the gentlemen of Clapton for 500 guineas and the Homerton club took on all comers from Hackney, Clapton and Stoke Newington for the same substantial sum.

58. *Angling on the River Lea. A watercolour by C. Bigot, c1840.*

59. *A fishery ticket for the White House, 1810.*

Keeping the Peace

AN EIGHTEENTH-CENTURY MAGISTRATE

The first newspaper reports available, in the 1720s, show that Hackney had its fair share of crime of all kinds, not to mention disputes between neighbours and between husband and wife. A focal point for all complaints was the local magistrate, Henry Norris, a substantial landowner in south Hackney. In an age when the Middlesex magistrates were notorious for their corruption, there is no evidence of Norris, a wealthy and conscientious churchman, having abused his office, or having treated it as anything other than a public service. Certainly, in between his courts at the Clerkenwell Sessions, he could expect to be roused at his house in Grove Street at any time, whether to deal with the committal of a serious criminal to Newgate, or to arbitrate on a neighbourhood brawl. Norris even fined his own coachman for swearing.

From his notebook of informal jottings, ten years' worth of which has survived, it is clear that Norris had to exercise the judgement of Solomon between parties brought before him in the heat of a dispute. This might involve a poultry thief caught in the act, a destitute wife seeking redress against an errant husband, an aggrieved parish official taking to task an indolent pauper, a dupe complaining of a confidence trickster, or a citizen assaulted by one of the locality's handful of regularly violent drunkards.

Swearing in public was not only a crime; in pious Hackney it caused great offence, and it seems to have been particularly rife among coach drivers. A campaign to enforce the statutes against their foul language was begun by respectable, dissenting Hackney in 1751, and echoed instantly by equally respectable and dissenting Stoke Newington (who thought the Hackney drivers were by far the worse).

Insults to reputation, particularly that of a woman, were regarded as an ecclesiastical offence, and there are instances recorded of men being made to stand in Hackney church during Sunday

60. Henry Norris's house, South Hackney, drawn by G.W. Toussaint c1845.

ELIZABETH CHIVERS, *in the agonies of despair,
throwing her Bastard Child into a Pond, near Hackney.*

*61. Numerous suicide attempts are recorded in Hackney
ponds, as well as the disposal of weapons by such as the
Gregory gang, with whom the deeply unpleasant
Richard Turpin associated. Here Elizabeth Chivers, who
was hanged for infanticide at Tyburn in 1712, is shown
in the sensational manner of the Newgate Calendar
disposing of her illegitimate daughter in what was
presumably Clapton Pond. 'Her father dying while she
was very young left her in indigent circumstances,
which obliged her to go into service when she was only
14 years of age ... she lived in several reputable families
in which her conduct was deemed irreproachable. When
she arrived at the age of almost 30 years she lived [at
Stepney] with one Mr Ward, an attorney, who prevailed
upon her to live with him; in consequence she bore the
child which she afterwards murdered.'*

service dressed in a white sheet to do penance for
slander.

If the magistrate before whom disputing parties
appeared could settle the matter on the spot, he
would. A petty offence might be followed by a
fine in favour of the parish poor (or some hours
in the stocks in default). An offender, before being
brought before the magistrate, might already have
cooled his heels in the parish cage for some hours,
and that might be regarded as punishment enough.

But if the magistrate took a more serious view
of the offence he would commit the prisoner to the
Clerkenwell bridewell (house of correction) for a
month or so. An offender might be ordered to
stand in the pillory as well as, or instead of, being
sent to prison: a deer-stealer, a young man arrested
in the grounds of Hackney House with 22 guineas
in his pocket in 1783, chose a day in the pillory
in preference to a year in prison. But to risk the
pillory was to risk one's life, as a culprit was
regarded as fair game for any missile the aggrieved
populace might throw.

Norris only occasionally came face to face with
a serious offender against property, and much
more rarely with instances of injury greater than
bruises received in a pub brawl. But his experi-
ences as a magistrate can only have informed his
decision, when he rebuilt his house in Grove Street
in 1729, to make massive provision for security,
in the form of iron bars on basement and ground
floor windows, and heavy locks on doors between
the staircase and the entrances to each floor. Only
weeks before his house was built, a family of local
farmers had been bound in the middle of the night
by a gang of robbers – soldiers who had taken off
their coats so as not to be identified by their regi-
mental badges.

The 1730s heralded the heyday of the highwayman. Norris committed to Newgate a deer-stealer
and burglar belonging to the brutal gang with
whom Dick Turpin associated. In 1737 Turpin
escaped arrest for horse-stealing in Whitechapel,
largely because he shot and killed one of his own
comrades, and hid out in a safe house in Hackney
Marsh (the White House, according to legend). He
ultimately found his way onto the gallows; others
of his kind, after execution at Tyburn, were exhib-
ited on the gibbet at Stamford Hill. Favourite
hunting grounds, whether for mounted robbers or
footpads, were surprisingly close to built up areas:
Cambridge Heath, the Hackney Road, and London
Fields in particular, attracted armed robbers.

62. *The Church House ('Urswick's House'), Hackney, the pillory and the parish cage.*

POLICING THE PARISH

In 1764 the seriousness of local crime led to the setting up of a more organised parish watch under special Act of Parliament. Undoubtedly the better street lighting which resulted improved safety on the road. But there were several instances, however, of gentlemen being robbed in their own gardens at pistol point, and the anxieties of the citizenry turned more towards thefts of property from their homes. In 1777, Hackney inhabitants collectively offered rewards for the apprehension and conviction of thieves, on a tariff which clearly indicates their priorities: £40 for the conviction of a burglar, £20 for a highwayman, £10 for a horse, lead or poultry thief and £2 for a sheep-stealer.

Towards the end of the century there are accounts of duels in Hackney, Homerton and Hoxton, between political opponents, and between a moneylender and his client. There was also a pistol fight in a Hackney dining room – this time over a lady's reputation.

The Hackney Association for the Preservation of Peace Liberty and Property was formed in the 1770s, and the presence of its volunteer militiamen was largely responsible for the area's escape from the effects of the Gordon Riots in 1780, which did widespread damage not only in London but in neighbouring villages. The Loyal Hackney Volunteers, as they came to be called, also seem to have acted as a reserve on whom the parish watchmen could call for assistance against everyday crime. After falling into a decline, the corps was re-formed in 1803, at the height of national alarm about a French invasion, and the two companies were augmented by a third, of riflemen. Local property owners were the principal sponsors of the corps and there was a strong whiff of class distinction about the whole thing: one of the companies was intended for gentlemen who could afford to pay for their own equipment, and another for those whose rifles, swords and greatcoats had to paid for out of public subscriptions – never sufficient once the threat of war had faded.

After the end of the French wars there was again a high incidence of crime, both highway robbery and burglary. In the 1820s a detachment of the Bow Street patrol was stationed in the parish, and attempts were made to increase the manpower and efficiency of the parish watchmen. These were the beginnings of a local police force, organised into two districts and divisions of ten men under an inspector, and equipped with greatcoats, lanterns, and cutlasses or truncheons. Carbines were kept in case of serious trouble. The patrols were disbanded on the formation of the Metropolitan Police in 1829.

Hackney Volunteer Riflemen.

THIS Corps having in Stock a few RIFLES and SWORDS, with the neceſſary Accoutrements, are ready to allow the Uſe of them, without Purchaſe, to any reſpeſtable Young Men who have the Good of their Country at Heart, and are willing to join this Corps; the ſame to be approved by the Committee, and to find their own Clothes, the Expence of which is very moderate.

₊ Applications to be made to Mr. IRELAND, Treaſurer to the Corps, Church-Street, Hackney.

63. Advertisement for the Loyal Hackney Volunteers, 1803.

64. A Hackney volunteer rifleman: a Rowlandson print of 1802.

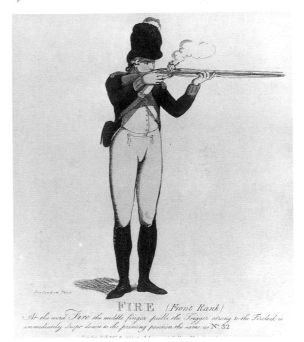

FIRE *(Front Rank)*
At the word *Fire the middle finger pulls the Trigger ſtrong & the Firelock is immediately dropt down to the priming poſition the ſame as* N.º 32

Refuge, Rescue and Retreat

ALMSHOUSES

Hackney's situation as a pleasant village close to the City made it, like its neighbour Shoreditch, a natural choice for establishing refuges for the aged or the infirm, or for the care of the insane (and, no doubt, inconvenient) relatives of the affluent. But Hackney's earliest charitable housing foundations were all designed for local people.

In the seventeenth century, three institutions (which continue to flourish) were founded by childless, local benefactors who established homes for the elderly poor, a common enough practice at the time, intended perhaps, to ensure remembrance and heavenly recognition. The earliest was the almshouses, endowed in 1666 by Dr William Spurstowe, vicar of Hackney, on land to the west of Mare Street, on which parts of Navarino, Wilton, Greenwood and Graham Roads now stand. Six poor widows were provided with one-roomed cottages on a site in what is now Sylvester Path, with a small open space in front, and a garden at the back. The almshouses were rebuilt in 1819 from the proceeds of the sale of brick earth from the endowed land; by the end of the century there were protests that the location of the almshouses, opposite a pub, was scarcely appropriate. An attractive new building in Navarino Road, with enlarged accommodation, was opened in 1966.

Almost as ancient a foundation is that of Henry Monger, owner of what, after his death, became the Cass estate in South Hackney. In 1669 he endowed almshouses for six 'poor, civil, honest' men of Hackney parish, which were built in Dutch style red-brick on the present site of Monger House in Church Crescent. A trust was administered by the heirs of Monger's friend and trustee, Thomas Cass, who, contrary to the terms of Monger's will,

65. *Spurstowe's Almshouses from Hackney Grove, looking north towards what is now Sylvester Path. The neighbourhood was Spurstowe's own property; he owned a large house on the approximate site of Gibbons' shop in Amhurst Road. A watercolour by George Hawkins.*

66. *Monger's Almshouses, Church Crescent, before rebuilding in 1847. By R. B. Schnebbelie.*

permitted the widows of almsmen to stay on in the houses after a husband's death, a practice which was stopped when the administration was taken over by the Rector and churchwardens of St John-at-Hackney in 1800. (Such widows were later given special preference when almshouses for women were built in memory of Henry Handley Norris, South Hackney's first rector, in Victoria Park Road in 1854.)

Bishop Wood's Almshouses, Hackney's third group of seventeenth-century almshouses are, uniquely, still in their original form. Founded in 1690 under the will of Dr Thomas Wood, Bishop of Lichfield and Coventry, they were built in an attractive location by Clapton Pond for poor widows aged over 60. Something of the reverent gentleman's motivation may be seen in his stipulation that inmates should have, every other year, a new gown with the initials 'T.W.' on the shoulders (the trustees soon chose to commute this to a money payment).

The West Hackney almshouses in Northwold Road have a more unusual history. The original house, containing eight apartments, was built by Thomas Cooke, a Turkey merchant and son of the one-time lord of the manor, shortly after 1740 on land enclosed from Stoke Newington Common on a 99-year lease. After Cooke's death in 1752 it was

found that the settlement was legally flawed, but Cooke's heirs continued to maintain the eight poor families rent-free in the house, despite having no obligation to do so. It seems that Cooke was particularly interested in the support of families with small children – this sets this bequest apart from the more usual charities for the elderly. New accommodation was built on the present site in 1889.

Of the succeeding generation of almshouses, several of which were in or near Retreat Place, nothing remains. The name of this street comes from the home, known as Robinson's (or the Widows') Retreat, for the widows of Independent and Baptist ministers; this was endowed by the architect, Samuel Robinson, in 1812. He and his wife were buried in the plot of ground in front of the attractive gothic building, on the south side of Retreat Place, although the grave was removed to Abney Park when the site was redeveloped.

The only almshouses built in Stoke Newington proper were single-storey brick dwellings on a Greek revival model, unusually spacious for almshouses, in Yoakley Road. These were established in 1835 out of funds bequeathed more than a century earlier by a Quaker, Michael Yoakley. The buildings were demolished in 1957.

The Victorian generation of almshouses began with a group of working jewellers in Clerkenwell,

67. *Robinson's Retreat almshouses, showing Robinson's tomb.*

who founded a charity for relief of poverty among their fellow tradespeople in 1827. The almshouse subscriptions began in 1840, resulting in a row of almshouses in Holcroft Road in 1853. The site was eventually absorbed into that for the Orchard Primary School. The Norris Memorial Almshouses, similar in style, were built in 1854 on the corner of Handley Road. Ostensibly a parish memorial, much of the funding came from the Norris family; the architect was Charles Parker. The buildings were demolished in 1968 and replaced by the sheltered housing of Norris Court.

By the end of the 1860s two further charities, this time concerned with groups of ethnic origin, had established homes for the aged poor. One was the creation of Emanuel Pacifico, who left money for almshouses to be administered by the Spanish and Portuguese Jews' congregation. These were established on the east side of London Fields, to be replaced by the London County Council's Darcy Buildings (now Darcy House) in 1904. The other, accommodating by far the largest number of any of the almshouses in Hackney of the seventeenth to nineteenth centuries, was an emanation of London's Huguenot community – Protestants who had fled religious persecution in France from 1686 onwards. This was the Hospital for Poor French Protestants, originally founded in Finsbury. Its sixty inmates were transferred from Bath Street to R.L. Roumieu's extraordinary red-brick French chateau in Victoria Park Road in 1865. The building was run on institutional lines, in contrast to almshouses where residents were expected to lead independent lives in their own separate dwellings. The hospital, with one of time's ironies, has since become a Roman Catholic school.

REFUGES

By the middle of the eighteenth century several of the area's large old houses, vacated by the wealthy, like Brooke House, were in institutional hands. In 1757, the press noted that Balmes House had been taken by 'an eminent physician', Meyer Schomberg, for the reception of lunatics. In the 1770s it was administered by Dr John Silvester and his partner Roger Devey, but by the 1820s it had passed to the far from eminent Thomas Warburton, who had worked his way up to marry the proprietor's widow, and who ran this and other establishments nearby with a mixture of bribery,

68. *The Goldsmiths' and Jewellers' Almshouses, Holcroft Road. There were eight places for men and eight for women. The building was designed by W.P. Griffith and widely admired in its day.*

69. *The French Hospital, Victoria Park Road (now the Cardinal Pole School annex).*

70. *Northumberland House, Woodberry Down in the 1840s.*

71. *The Deaf and Dumb Asylum, 179 Lower Clapton Road. Built by a pottery manufacturer who had made his fortune from chamber pots depicting the trial of Dr Sacheverell in 1710, the house was known locally as Pisspot Hall.*

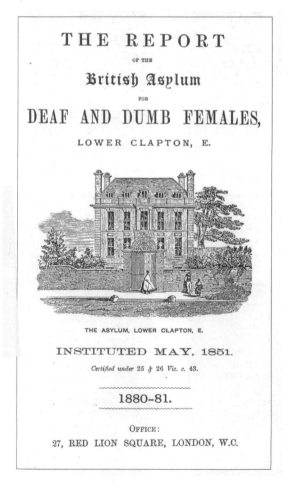

nepotism, starvation and violence. Warburton himself was a heavy, tall man with a countenance that terrified George III. 'Take away that fellow with the long nose – take him away! Away! Away', the King is alleged to have said on seeing Warburton at Windsor.

In 1818 the East India Company entered into an arrangement with Dr Rees, for the reception at Pembroke House of employees certified insane while serving in India. This house was set in substantial grounds on the west side of Mare Street. Rees charged rates which depended on whether the employee was a first class patient (officers and senior civil servants) at £100 a year, or not, in which case the fee fell to £40. The asylum remained open until 1870, when the land was taken by the Great Eastern Railway and developed as Bayford Street.

More rural delights were offered to the private patients of Northumberland House, Green Lanes. This house had been built in 1822-24 by Stephen Cundee of Islington, and so named probably because a builder relative of his had worked in the Duke of Northumberland's London houses. By 1835, it also had become an asylum for the mentally ill: its prospectus made the most of the views over three counties and the pleasant walks to the villages of Tottenham, Highgate and Southgate. Like Pembroke House, it offered differential rates, but was more costly, at up to 5 guineas a week. Northumberland House was in use for psychiatric patients until 1954, when it was demolished for the building of Rowley Gardens on the Woodberry Down estate.

In 1783 Thomas Braidwood of Edinburgh, who had developed new techniques for teaching the deaf, took an old house, Bowling Green House (by a former bowling green) on what later became Chatham Place. He renamed the house Grove House and established his new Academy for the Deaf and Dumb, where one of the pupils was an illegitimate son of Charles James Fox. The enterprise was carried on, after Braidwood's health failed, by other members of his family at Pembroke House and then at Cambridge Heath. The longer-lived British Asylum for Deaf and Dumb Females began in small premises on Stamford Hill in 1851, moving to the old-fashioned and dilapidated Eagle House, Homerton in 1857. By 1860 the charity was established in one of Hackney's handsomest Georgian houses, no. 179 Lower Clapton Road, and housed women from the very young to the very old. This house was compulsorily purchased and demolished in 1930, when the home moved to Clapton Common where it survived until about 1986.

A unique institution, founded in Jewry Street in

72. *Ayahs outside the Ayahs' Home, 26 King Edward's Road, c1910.*

the City, was moved in 1900 to 26 King Edward's Road, a substantial house of the 1870s but (as a product of the Freehold Land Society development of Warneford and Fremont Streets described on page 98) in a different league from the antiquity or grandeur of such as Brooke House or the Deaf and Dumb Asylum. This was the London City Mission's Ayahs' Home, whose aim was to accommodate the women from India or, frequently, even further east, who were employed to look after the children of expatriate English families, and who might be paid for their valued services in taking charge of children throughout a voyage home, but dismissed and left, friendless, in the riverside districts, to look for new employment once their employers had reached home ground. It might take them weeks or months to find further employment, and meanwhile they were vulnerable to exploitation of all kinds. The Home, which tended to accommodate up to 100 inmates a year, later moved to no. 4 King Edward's Road, and closed during the last war.

RESCUE WORK

Hackney School at Lower Clapton, which closed in 1819, made way for Hackney's only purpose-built refuge, the London Orphan Asylum, a charity founded a few years earlier in the East End by Andrew Reed. It was designed to help destitute children with no living parent, or with an impoverished mother, and who might need to be rescued 'from the walks of vice and profligacy'. Admission depended on the patronage of a subscriber, and was balloted for, candidates having demonstrated that their families were 'respectable'. They were disqualified if they had any association with the workhouse. The Asylum, later the London Orphan School, left Clapton after a cholera outbreak in 1866, moving to Watford, where, in 1915, it changed its name to Reed's School. The Salvation Army took over the premises for its Congress Hall, and Linscott Road was built over the forecourt. At Dalston, another orphanage with similar social limitations was founded, also by Reed, in 1827. It moved out in 1843, becoming the Royal Wanstead School.

Another group of institutions were designed to accommodate young women who had drifted into prostitution, or were thought to be in need of re-

73. *The London Orphan Asylum from the Lower Clapton Road, depicted in 1826 by George Hawkins.*

74. Mission work in Haggerston, from a temperance magazine, c1850.

75. The Waterloo Rooms, a mission house in Prout Road, c1930.

straint 'from deviating from the path of virtue'. The earliest of these associated with the area, which insisted on its inmates demonstrating sincere penitence before finding them steady work, was the London Female Penitentiary ('in no sense should it be confounded with a place of detention', said its fundraisers). Established in Pentonville in 1807, it moved in 1884 to no. 191 High Street, Stoke Newington. It was financed partly through the 'betrayed and fallen young women' operating a steam laundry for 'persons who sympathise with rescue work'.

A short-lived establishment with similar objectives was founded in 1829 in Grove Street (Lauriston Road) by a group of Hackney residents. Despite the support of the Home Secretary, Robert Peel, it was dissolved 'through the misconduct of one of its officers'. Its work was, however, carried on by the British Penitent Female Refuge, under royal patronage, which began in the Hackney Road in the same year, moving subsequently to Bethnal Green and then in 1842 to Cambridge Heath, to a house in Andrews Road. Its façade survives, fronting premises rebuilt for the Cintique chair works. The Refuge mutated into an industrial (reformatory) school for girls.

A refuge for the destitute, which in practice seems to have accommodated mainly young discharged prisoners of both sexes, had been established in the Hackney Road in 1811, moving to Dalston in 1849. The women earned a living by taking in laundry from institutions and private families, and the men from tailoring, carpentry and shoemaking. Another home for discharged women prisoners was the Elizabeth Fry Refuge, which opened in 1860 and ran for over half a century at no. 195 Mare Street (presently the Lansdowne Club), a rare survival of the type of town house that in the nineteenth century so frequently came to shelter the afflicted and the unfortunate.

In the later nineteenth century, mission work was pursued amongst the labouring poor by all denominations. The Salvation Army was founded while William Booth was living in a now-demolished house in Gore Road. Apart from taking over several old houses as hostels, among them the Ivy House (where the Mothers' Hospital for unmarried pregnant women began in 1884), the Army's training headquarters moved in to the building that had formerly been the London Orphan Asylum. Despite the well-meaning efforts of middle-class temperance workers, such as are depicted rosily in illustration 74, by the 1890s the social researcher Charles Booth concluded that in Hackney the temperance movement had been a total failure.

76. Houses adjoining Stoke Newington churchyard. A watercolour by T.H. Shepherd, 1843.

Town Terraces and Country Villas

When John Rocque published his parish survey in 1745, Hackney was still characterised by its houses, both ancient and modern, having been built in a haphazard way, each for a particular landowner, according to the fashion of the time. Apart from the Tyssens' own house at Shacklewell, and Bishop Wood's house north of Clapton Pond (later the home of the influential Powell family), the late-seventeenth and early-eighteenth century had seen some splendid and substantial building for wealthy citizens in South Hackney, and at the west end of Homerton, and Lower Clapton, where 'the Five Houses' on part of the former grounds of Hackney House, east of the main road, named a neighbourhood that survived the houses themselves.

In Stoke Newington also, where more early-eighteenth-century building survives, houses were put up singly or in small batches, especially along Church Street and the High Street. A notable and special development consisted of the Palatine houses, built on the west side of Stoke Newington High Street from 1710 onwards, following a parish commitment to house four families of refugees from Germany. These were constructed in that part of the area which was a detached part of Hornsey parish.

From the 1770s there was a trend towards more systematic development, still on a small scale, but of urban, terraced houses of a kind designed to appeal – as being familiar – to the London resident who wanted City comforts without its noise and smells. Among the first such attractions was Clapton Terrace, built about 1777 on the west side of the Common, along with its own proprietary chapel, by a Mr Devall. Like Sanford Terrace, built on land acquired in 1776 by a brewer called (and spelled) Sandford, they consist of similar, but not identical, houses constructed in a row, rather than

77. *Map of Stoke Newington, 1855.*

of an architectural composition designed to be considered as a whole. Similar were the earliest houses built in St Thomas's Square, east of Mare Street. These, built by Robert Collins senior from 1771 on the 'East field' belonging to St Thomas's Hospital, fell victim to comprehensive redevelopment.

More self-conscious in design were the palace-fronted Hackney Terrace (nos. 20-54 Cassland Road) built from 1792 by a triumvirate of City speculators out of subscriptions from building tradesmen; and Buccleuch Terrace (illustration 80), a tragic loss, built in 1826 north east of Clapton Common on land belonging to Samuel Tyssen.

A similar contrast can be seen between Sutton Place, first occupied in 1809, and its contemporary, The Paragon, in Paragon Road. Though the builder, the energetic Robert Collins, was the same in both cases, in the latter terrace, reminiscent in its arcading and side porches of Michael Searles's Paragon at Blackheath, and with its distinctive arabesque fanlights, he was working to an architect's design. Indeed in 1803 'Mr Collins, carpenter, Mare Street' had sought investors by advertising a site in Chatham Place, to be built in crescent form and 'in an architectural stile'. This might have been either the Paragon or the similarly sized houses put up on the west side of Chatham Place, except that neither, in the result, was built as a crescent. The Collins family also built in Hackney Grove, developed in the 1780s, but on a more piecemeal basis.

After Buccleuch Terrace, and the contemporary Clapton Square, also on Tyssen land, and much similar terraced housing which lined Kingsland Road and Dalston Lane, developed by the Rhodes family, the emphasis changed to building detached and grander villas. Thus from 1820 onwards, Upper Clapton was developed more or less as a villa suburb by W.G. Daniel Tyssen (who, born W.G. Daniel, had taken the surname of his wife). Remarkable amongst the many substantial villas were Craven Lodge, home of the Craven family and later of the politician and philanthropist Samuel Morley, whose ivy-clad folly still stands on the Tower estate at Stamford Hill; and Gothic Hall, on the east side of Stamford Hill, built for the Windus family, who are commemorated in the road of that name. But the pointer to the future had come with the lease in 1777 by Joshua Hobson of a large brickfield at Kingsland. By 1830, the area between Kingsland Road and London Fields, and creeping ever northwards, was a vast brickfield, in the hands of the farmer-turned-builder William Rhodes.

78. Palatine House, Palatine Avenue. Built in the mid-eighteenth century, the house was used as a retreat in the 1780s by John Wesley. Drawn by Florence Bagust in 1915.

79. Church Row, on the north side of Stoke Newington Church Street. A watercolour by T.H. Shepherd, 1843.

80. Buccleuch Terrace.

81. Newington Hall, on the present site of Statham Grove, c1850. Lithograph by Dean and Munday.

82. *Brickfields in the Kingsland Road, imagined by the watercolourist C. H. Matthews, c. 1850, to illustrate descriptive verse written in 1800 by William Fox the Younger, a City merchant.*

83. *Brick kilns at Upper Clapton, from the river, c1830.*

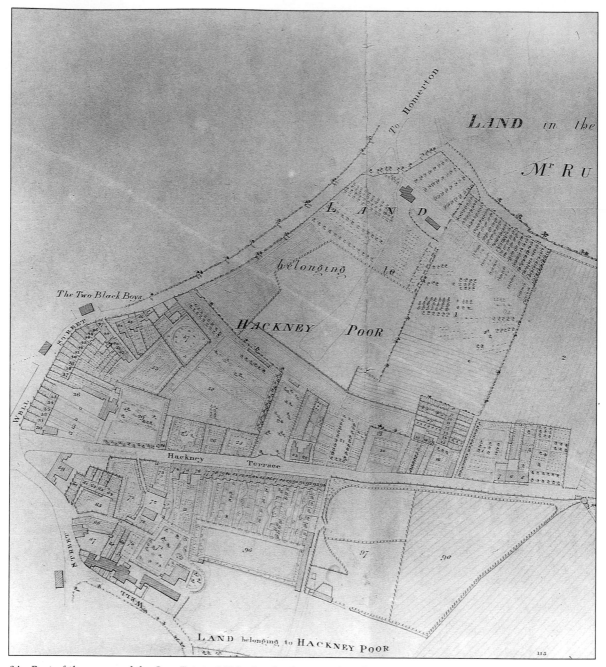

84. *Part of the survey of the Cass Estate, 1806, showing layouts of gardens at Hackney Terrace (20-54 Cassland Road) and the 'pleasure grounds' behind the terrace. The large house (no. 71) on the present site of Meynell Gardens, was a boys' school. Monger's almshouses, shown on the plan to the south west of this house, were rebuilt in 1847. Surveyor, Jesse Gibson.*

85. *Cintra Cottage stood on the east side of Lordship Road, opposite its junction with Woodberry Down. This music was published before 1833.*

86. *Gothic Hall, the home of Thomas Windus, FSA, after whose family Windus Road is named (it was formerly Birdcage Walk, after the pub on the corner of Stamford Hill). The 'Hall' stood on the east side of Stamford Hill, on the site of Berwyn House. Windus constructed and furnished the museum annexed to his house, seen here on the left of the picture, in the style of a chapel of the time of Henry VIII. It housed an eclectic collection of ancient sculptures, coins and metalwork, and several hundred Old Master drawings, 'gathered together', said the local antiquarian Dr Benjamin Clarke, 'in an eccentric fashion, [and] in like manner dispersed'.*

87. *A room in Gothic Hall.*

Hackney and Stoke Newington At Prayer

88. Anna (or Hannah) Trapnel. An eighteenth-century print, original by Gaywood.

89. St Thomas's Square Chapel, often known simply as Hackney Chapel. Lithograph by H.F. Hamon and F. Ireland, c1850.

EARLY DISSENTERS

From an early date Hackney, perhaps on account of its proximity to, yet separation from the City, was known as a place of relative toleration for those who could not accept the teachings of the Church of England. Numerous dissenting congregations set up here. Hackney was home to the preacher and prophetess Anna Trapnel, who was imprisoned by Cromwell's government for seditious criticism of the Protectorate. A manuscript in the British Library records that, in 1683, although there were three or four unlawful 'conventicles' in Hackney, they had all been 'suppressed'. The suppression did not last.

Congregations would form and then find themselves divided by doctrinal differences; as a result, they prove too many to enumerate here. The earliest recorded dissenters were a group of Presbyterians, established before 1636, on the west side of Mare Street. After a contested election for their minister in 1715, the losing faction broke away and established the Old Gravel Pit Meeting House at the north-east end of Chatham Place, on

90. Joseph Priestley.

91. Daniel Defoe.

what had been the Gravel Pit Field.

Then, the original congregation moved across the street, building St Thomas's Square Chapel in 1777 and enlarging it in 1824. The attribution to St Thomas is a purely topographical one, the ground landlord being St Thomas's Hospital. The fabric of the chapel was incorporated into the cinema (later a bingo hall) which stood on the site until 1996, when it was demolished to make way for new accommodation for Cordwainers' College. The gateway to their burial ground still stands, however, to the south. The surviving memorials include one, close to the gateway, to Thomas Braidwood, the pioneer teacher of the deaf.

Dr Joseph Priestley, the eminent scientist who discovered oxygen, and who was also a radical political philosopher and theologian, became minister of the breakaway Gravel Pit congregation in 1791, succeeding his friend Dr Richard Price. Priestley had been vilified for his espousal of the libertarian principles of the French Revolution, and Hackney provided a refuge from the anti-republican mob who had driven him from Birmingham, and destroyed his chapel, home and laboratory there. In radical Hackney, Priestley was as secure as he was ever likely to be in England. At New College, established in Stamp Brooksbank's former Hackney House about 1786, Priestley taught religious and scientific subjects to student ministers. But his presence was a cause of disquiet to those local people who perceived themselves patriots, not least when he was made an honorary French citizen. He himself found the fervent atmosphere in which the Loyal Hackney Volunteers were established more than enough to make him uneasy. In 1794 he followed his sons to the freer atmosphere of America, never to return.

In 1810 there were fears for the stability of the Old Chapel, which had been constructed in 1715, and a new building, inevitably known as the New Gravel Pit Chapel, rose on a new site, abutting Chatham Place on its eastern side. This was during the ministry of the extremely popular preacher Dr Robert Aspland. Ironically, it was soon after his death, in 1845, that a still larger building was planned, and a Gothic church designed by Henry Darbishire took its place in 1858 just as the congregation began a long and slow decline. Darbishire's church was demolished in 1970, but part of its burial ground survives to the west of Mead Place.

OTHER NON-CONFORMISTS

Other non-conformists included a group of congregationalists which moved into the Old Gravel Pit; eventually this flourishing congrega-

92. Interior of the Old Gravel Pit Chapel, before alterations in its Congregationalist days, in 1852.

93. The New Gravel Pit Chapel in Chatham Place, 1810. The Unitarian philosophy was encapsulated in an entablature on its frontage: 'Sacred to one God, the Father'.

tion secured a much enlarged site in Lower Clapton Road. Here, in 1868, they built the remarkable Round Chapel, still one of Hackney's major landmarks. Then, a third group of congregationalists moved into the Old Gravel Pit and this original building, though barely recognisable today as a chapel in its twentieth-century factory guise, is the only one of Hackney's earliest dissenting meeting houses to survive. Ironically, one of the reasons the Unitarians moved out of it in 1810 was because they thought it was unsafe.

The Kingsland Congregational church is notable for tracing its beginnings to a mission founded for the large numbers working in brick-making in the area in 1789. Another chapel, originally an iron structure, was built at Cambridge Heath in 1860. Its bells proved intolerable to the family of Salvation Army founder, General William Booth, who found themselves obliged to move from the neighbourhood to Gore Road. Iron chapels were a common expedient as a stopgap in the mid-nineteenth century. St Mark's, St Mary of Eton and St Matthew's at Upper Clapton all first took this form. Another was built in Dalston Lane, opposite Graham Road, for a congregation who seceded

from St Philip's in Richmond Road, and was later replaced by St Bartholomew's. Hackney's only surviving iron church is in Shrubland Road. It was bought off-the-peg from the catalogue of a Moorgate firm, and put up in ten weeks in 1858 for 'English Presbyterians' (congregationalists), whom it housed until they merged with Trinity Chapel in South Hackney in 1971. On the death of its most charismatic nineteenth-century minister, Thomas Udall (1878-1909), the fabric was estimated to have a further life expectancy of 25 years; but it is still there, since about 1970 in the hands of an evangelical congregation.

The Baptists were first noted in Hackney in 1641, when a group of itinerants were recorded as having arrived in the Marshes. They scandalised conforming parishioners by baptising each other in the Lea. By the end of the century, however, a permanent Baptist congregation had been founded in a former schoolroom in what is now Shore Road. With the arrival in 1811 of Dr F.A. Cox, an extremely popular preacher, they were obliged by force of numbers to move, choosing a site on the west side of Mare Street, just south of Helmsley Street. In 1854 a magnificent building was put up

94. *The Round Chapel, Lower Clapton Road, opened in 1868. For many years at risk, the Hackney Historic Buildings Trust has secured it a new future as a performance and rehearsal space, opened in 1996.*

here by W.G. and E. Habershon, after a disastrous fire had destroyed its predecessor. Here the congregation remained until bomb damage moved them out; Frampton Park Road church was built as a replacement in 1956.

When the Baptists left the Shore Place chapel the Methodists moved in, though not for long, as larger premises were found in Paragon Road within a few years, and themselves enlarged in 1825. The congregation moved to Richmond Road in 1846. But like all these denominations, as the century progressed new congregations sprang up in newly colonised areas of the borough.

One of the smaller, unique Hackney chapels stood in Well Street. It was established in 1800 on a site facing westwards from the westernmost tip of Cassland Road. It was associated with a training institution for ministers and missionaries, the Evangelical Association for the Propagation of the Gospel, also known as the Village Itinerant Society, founded in 1803 by George Collison. In 1843 new college premises were built on the site of the present Orchard School, whence the Hackney Theological Seminary, as it came to be known, moved to Hampstead in 1887. The

building was taken over as overspill accommodation for the Bethnal Green workhouse.

In the 1790s, at a time when Protestant dissenters had a choice of four places of worship, the fourteen families identified in Hackney as adhering to Rome had none. Their number grew, and in the 1840s services were held, before a church was built, in a disused brewery building behind the Two Black Boys pub. St John the Baptist, in King Edward's Road, was consecrated in 1848, its congregation at that time about 300. It was followed in 1856 by Our Lady and St Joseph in Tottenham Road, a building conversion in which A.W.N. Pugin himself had a hand. St Scholastica's, in Kenninghall Road, was associated with the Retreat, almshouses founded in the early 1860s by the Harrison family. The Immaculate Heart in Kenworthy Road began as a mission church in 1873.

Hackney's most notorious sect was housed in the Agapemonite Church in Rookwood Road, near Clapton Common. It was opened in 1896 as an offshoot of the so-called Agapemone, or 'Abode of Love', founded at Spaxton in Somerset by Henry Prince. Prince styled himself 'the Second Messiah', and promised his (mainly rich and female)

95. Newington Green Chapel, 1843, by T.H. Shepherd.

adherents eternal salvation of the body as well as the soul. He survived some serious sexual scandals, but being, contrary to his claims, less than immortal, his mantle descended on J.H. Smyth-Pigott, who caused a riot in 1902 by proclaiming his own deity from the Upper Clapton pulpit. He had subsequently to be rescued by the police from immersion in Clapton pond, where he had been taken by the mob to prove whether he could walk on water. The active life of the Clapton congregation could not, and did not, long survive this. Their remarkable building passed to the Church of the Good Shepherd, whose emphasis on the animal world makes the exterior sculptures of the beasts of Revelations seem particularly appropriate.

THE ESTABLISHED CHURCH EXPANDS

In 1726, Stephen Ram, who had bought Sir Thomas Cooke's former Homerton estate in 1722, fell out with the rector and churchwardens of Hackney church over his entitlement to a particular pew, and founded his own chapel, which stood in his grounds at the north-west end of Homerton High Street. After his death the building continued as a proprietary chapel, until demolished early this century.

By the beginning of the nineteenth century even the vast capacity of the new church of St John-at-Hackney was insufficient for the expanding population. The first chapel-of-ease, of modest size and of a simple classical design, was established in Well Street, South Hackney, in 1809, largely paid for by donations by the local landowning families. It was dedicated to St John of Jerusalem in commemoration of the former connection of the area with the Order of St John. When South Hackney became an independent parish after 1825, the local squire, Henry Handley Norris, then a curate of St John-at-Hackney, became its first rector. By the 1840s further development of the area meant that the chapel was already too small, and in 1847 the new church of St John of Jerusalem, in what is now Lauriston Road, was begun.

The other parish carved out when Hackney was being ecclesiastically rearranged, was West Hackney. It had its own church, on the east side of Stoke Newington Road as it becomes Stoke Newington High Street. Like a Greek temple in style, and designed by Sir Robert Smirke, it was opened in 1824; it could accommodate up to 2,000 people. Sadly, it was so badly damaged during the last war that no serious public effort was made to save it.

96. West Hackney Church, Stoke Newington High Street, 1841.

97. A confirmation service in St John-at-Hackney, c1840. Lithograph by George Hawkins.

In 1827 the parish also acquired and enlarged St Thomas's, at Clapton Common, which had been privately built in 1777 in association with the construction of Clapton Terrace. The prime movers in this transaction included the then rector, Archdeacon John Watson, and his brother Joshua, who had retired from a successful career as a wine merchant in the City to devote his life to Church matters. These two and H.H. Norris were at the centre of an influential High Church group, often called the 'Hackney Phalanx', which was closely involved in the movement to promote church schools, and opposed to non-denominational religious instruction. Religious life in Hackney in the 1830s and 1840s was dominated by the firm views of this group and the many issues on which they and the prominent dissenting ministers disagreed.

Always contentious were the church rates. The law made all property-holders liable to pay towards the upkeep of the parish church, whether or not they adhered to that church.

Matters came to a head in the 1830s in Hackney as elsewhere, although Hackney may have been unusual in that both the beadle and the church organist had to be laid off for a time as there was no money in the parish coffers to pay them. In West Hackney, the authorities attempted to enforce payment by levying distress against individuals' household goods. The seizure of one Mr Clarke's music stool became a *cause célèbre*, and brought such ridicule on the vestry that they never again attempted to raise a church rate. In Hackney itself a court case was brought against a carpenter called Nunn for the princely sum of 3 shillings and 4 pence. The parish incurred hundreds of pounds in costs, and poor Nunn lost his reason. In South Hackney there was a pragmatic truce: a church rate was set but payment was in practice voluntary. By the time Parliament finally abolished the rate, in 1868, the battle had long been over.

The acceleration of development after the 1840s required the building of many new churches; the earliest was St Barnabas, Homerton, 1847, by the local architect W.H. Ashpitel, resident in Clapton Square. By the First World War there were twenty four Anglican parishes, some with separate outreach missions. From the perspective of the present day, parishes appear to have divided and sub-divided, only to re-form, like the shapes in a kaleidoscope, after building damage in war time and in response to demographic change. There are some fifteen today.

98. A political meeting at the Mermaid, 1796, drawn by Gillray. MPs Byng and Fox addressing Middlesex freeholders against Government bills restricting freedom of assembly and speech.

Politics, Paupers and Patients

GOVERNMENT BY A FEW

Before 1613 all male parishioners of Hackney had been entitled to take part in the management of parish affairs at open vestry meetings. In that year, however, the Bishop of London, at the instigation of the wealthier residents who were concerned at the increasing influx of City tradesmen into the parish, created a self-perpetuating select vestry, consisting of no more than 32 parishioners as well as the clergy and churchwardens, to govern the parish.

Perhaps surprisingly, in view of this beginning, the select vestry co-existed more or less amicably, for more than two hundred years, with the parish meeting, held several times a year as occasion required, which all adult male inhabitants were entitled to attend and vote in. Although the select vestry functioned to a large extent as the executive of this parish meeting, which appointed its clerk, churchwardens and other officers, from the mid-eighteenth century special offices were created by local Acts of Parliament. These officials existed alongside the vestry, and managed specific tasks, such as the workhouse, the local constabulary and street lighting. The parish meeting continued to appoint the unpaid traditional officials, such as the Surveyor of Highways. It was common in Hackney, as it was in Stoke Newington, for a busy or wealthy appointee to pay a fine for refusing to serve in one of these positions, or to appoint a deputy to serve in his place. The parish meeting also appointed committees from time to time to look into matters of particular concern, such as encroachment on common lands, and to make representations on the inhabitants' behalf.

In the political climate of 1832, however, when government by ancient but undemocratic elites was being questioned in spheres from parliament downwards, there was a challenge to the legality of Hackney's select vestry, to which it offered no serious resistance. Control of parish affairs then reverted to the ratepayers at large, until the reorganisation of London government in 1855 effected a separation between the civil and the ecclesiastical parish.

The smaller population of Stoke Newington made extensive use of committees to deal with special problems, but was always constituted as an open vestry. And, as in Hackney, much work was done by paid officials or by more or less reluctant inhabitants elected to specific offices at regular vestry meetings. Some offices, such as those of vestry clerk and sexton, seem at various times to have descended on a hereditary basis from father to son, although for a time, at the beginning of the nineteenth century, the office of sexton was regularly held by a woman, and seems to have been regarded as a way of assisting a poor widow to earn a living.

CARING FOR THE POOR

In very early times provision for the care and welfare of the poor was made by the church or by voluntary contributions. From the early-seventeenth century care of those who were too old or feeble to look after themselves was the responsibility of the parish authorities, and usually took the form of money payments, or 'out-relief'.

But in the early-eighteenth century, concern that this could lead the 'able-bodied' poor to be an undue burden on the rate-paying populace led Hackney, as it did other growing communities

99. The north (street) front of the Hackney workhouse: a watercolour of the 1830s by B. Saunders. The premises, on the south side of Homerton High Street, later formed the nucleus of the Hackney Hospital. In this picture the front wall has been 'dropped' to enable the viewer to see the building properly.

close to London, to the establishment of work-houses. Here the aged, sick and infirm could be brought for attention, and those willing to work might have the profits from their labour recycled for the benefit of those subsidising their support. At the same time, the system legitimised the denial of out-relief to those found to be unwilling to work in the workhouse, and thereby characterised as 'undeserving'. The whole aim was to control expenditure and ease the burden on rate-payers.

Hackney established its first workhouse by rent-ing private premises in 1732, moving in 1741 to a house on the south side of Homerton High Street – at the extreme east, and in one of the least populated parts, of the parish. From an early date the business of the daily care of the inmates was farmed out, the contractor agreeing to feed each person and give them a change of linen for a fee of 2s 4d (12p) weekly. Eventually the authorities were unhappy with the service delivered, and in 1765 the parish took direct control of the premises, appointing a salaried workhouse master. Rope and twine-making, needlework, oakum picking and flax- and wool-spinning were taken in for the inmates to earn their keep.

The rules for the conduct of the establishment – set by parish government, and binding on in-mates and management alike – show that the fare provided was intended to be of reasonable quan-tity. There was to be a regular inspection of its

adequacy by the parish overseers, who were de-barred from being in the provisions trade. Some of their advertisements for butchers' tenders sur-vive, requiring substantial, if not necessarily prime, cuts of meat: 'mouse buttocks [hindleg of beef], thick flanks, clods, stickings (all to be delivered clear of bone); legs and shins of good ox beef; legs, breasts, shoulders and necks of good mutton'.

By the beginning of the nineteenth century the accommodation, adequate for thirty when first established, was housing nearly ten times as many, and the clergy were pressing for rebuilding. Control within the workhouse was such that numerous illegitimate children were conceived there, and the unsupervised inmates could come and go at will through the unrepaired walls. The inadequate and insanitary premises were not rebuilt until 1838, four years after Hackney and Stoke Newington had been joined in a Poor Law Union. This new building came to form part of the old Hackney Hospital.

In Stoke Newington, a house was leased in Church Street to serve as a workhouse in 1734, and until 1820 this accommodated between ten and twenty paupers: refusing to move in there would mean a reduction in any 'out relief' that would otherwise be paid. From time to time paupers would, for the sake of economy, be farmed out to private contractors, originally at Waltham Cross, and later at Mile End.

100. The south front of Hackney workhouse, a watercolour of the 1830s by B. Saunders.

It was in part the small numbers with which Stoke Newington had to deal that led in 1834 to its being joined with Hackney in matters of poor relief; it thenceforth sent its poor, who had no other settled home, to the workhouse in Homerton. The remoteness of this site, and the fact that Stoke Newington's share of the expenses was fixed at a tenth, although frequently the demand it made on the accommodation would have justified only half of that, was the cause of continuing resentment in the parish, so much so that by 1922 it could be claimed that 'it would be cheaper to send our paupers to the Hotel Cecil than to subscribe to Hackney Union'.

FROM CHURCH HOUSE TO TOWN HALL

In Stoke Newington the vestry had moved from meeting in the vestry house into the church itself, and then to the vestry room. In Hackney it might be necessary to hold the parish meeting at the Mermaid or the Assembly Rooms, but the smaller gatherings of the select vestry or the numerous boards and committees could be comfortably accommodated in the sixteenth-century Church House (illustration 62). This building reached the end of its repairable life in 1802 when it was replaced by the Old Town Hall (now bank premises) beside the old church tower.

Other activities occupied part of the town hall premises. In 1818, a savings bank was opened here

The rules governing Hackney's first workhouse were comprehensive. They included:

That no person of either Sex be allowed to smoke in Bed, or in any Bed-chamber of the House.

That a Bell be rung every Morning, in the Summer ... by Five, for the healthful People to rise to work; and to go to Bed in the Summer by Nine, and in the Winter by Eight, and the Mistress sees all the Candles out at those Times.

That all Persons, who through Idleness may pretend themselves Sick, Lame, or Infirm, so as to be excused their Working; such Imposters so discovered, either by their Stomachs or the Apothecary, shall be carried before a Magistrate, in order to be punished as the Law directs.

101. *The new Hackney Town Hall of 1865. It was demolished once the present Town Hall, built behind it, was ready for use, and its site became an open forecourt.*

for 'tradesmen, mechanics, servants, labourers and others', and here in 1837, the first civil registry of births, deaths and marriages opened its doors. Also, the parish fire engine was kept on the premises.

By the time the municipal vestry, and Board of Works for Hackney and Stoke Newington, with their enlarged responsibilities for building control, sanitation and roads, were created in 1855 under the Metropolis Management Act, still more office and committee space was required. (In this re-organisation Stoke Newington became one of eight wards of the new Hackney district and its new, and select, vestry met locally, often in the parish schoolroom.) One proposal for a new Hackney Town Hall involved the charming idea of incorporating the old St Augustine's church tower into a suitably Gothic municipal building. A larger site was, however, inevitable and so the new building of 1866 occupied what had formerly been the open space in front of the Georgian houses of Hackney Grove. When the modern Town Hall was built, this became an open space again. After Stoke Newington achieved separate status in 1894, its vestry offices occupied the handsome 1881 building of South Hornsey district council in Milton Grove. These were extended in 1915, but the site was never going to be adequate for the metropoli-

tan borough which was formed to supersede both Stoke Newington and South Hornsey in 1900, and it found its first purpose-built home in a new complex built on the site of Church Row in Church Street in 1937.

CARING FOR THE SICK

Although the workhouses offered accommodation for the invalid poor, caring otherwise for the sick was mainly the work of philanthropic and private institutions. In Stoke Newington, two such enterprises were neighbours. The Dispensary, founded in 1825 and housed with its resident physician from 1862 at no. 189 High Street, was next door to the Invalid Female Asylum to the south, whose work was emphatically amongst single and 'respectable' servants and shop-assistants. The Lock Hospital at Kingsland, the old Leper Hospital, was seemingly used later for a wider range of patients, but ceased to be used as a hospital in the middle of the eighteenth century. Thereafter the nearest hospital provision on any scale was at the London Hospital in Whitechapel, a charitable foundation of 1765, some of whose physicians lived in Hackney, and at St Bartholomew's in Smithfield, with which the Lock Hospital had always been associated.

102. *The new buildings of the German Hospital, 1864, by T.L. Donaldson, replacing the Georgian mansion into which the Hospital had first moved in 1845.*

103. *Poster for a protest meeting, 1892.*

By 1845 the German Hospital – unlike its French counterpart, truly a hospital in the modern sense – was established at Dalston, on the former premises of the Infant Orphan Asylum. Most of its out-patients and casualty cases were consistently drawn from the local, indigenous community rather than from the German-speaking residents of London whom it had been established to serve.

There was no large general hospital in the area until the arrival of the Metropolitan Hospital in Kingsland Road in 1885. By this time the Metropolitan was half a century old, since it had been founded earlier in Lincoln's Inn Fields, and had gradually moved north east, coming to Dalston only reluctantly, as the site was perceived to be too near to the German Hospital.

Most hospitals would not accept tuberculosis cases, and so, in 1851, the recently founded City of London Hospital for Diseases of the Chest, also a result of a private initiative begun in the City, began building on a site in Bonner Road, on the south side of the newly opened Victoria Park. This was the first building on the extensive ground acquired by the Crown for building round the Park itself.

It was becoming clear, not least because of the cholera and typhoid epidemics of mid-nineteenth century London, that the workhouses were unable to cope with the proper care of the invalid poor.

104. Interior of a ward in St Joseph's Hospice, 1915.

In 1868 new legislation required the poor law authorities to establish separate wards for hospital treatment – Hackney's was in Gainsborough Road. The Act also set up the Metropolitan Asylums Board to establish and administer special hospitals – the government insisted in the face of criticism on calling them 'asylums' – to deal with mental illness and with cases of fever and smallpox.

The Asylums Board, like the governors of the French Hospital and the Chest Hospital before it, chose the area of Victoria Park as one of three sites within London for its fever and smallpox hospitals. The work on opening the wards was given a special impetus by the known approach of a smallpox epidemic, and the Homerton site (now that of the modern Homerton Hospital) was opened in 1871, treating over 2,600 cases in its first fifteen months, sometimes having to resort to the corridors to find room for the number of patients needing admission. The smallpox and fever sections of the hospital were deliberately physically separated. A plan to site a further smallpox hospital at Stoke Newington met with local protest, in unconscious echo of Hackney in 1768; it was built at Tottenham instead.

A group of Roman Catholic nuns, the Irish Sisters of Charity, established themselves in Mare Street about 1900, to supply home nursing for the terminally ill amongst the local working population. A benefactor made them a gift of Cambridge Lodge Villas, enabling them to care for in-patients also. From that time, St Joseph's Hospice, as it became, has been in the forefront of the hospice movement, gradually expanding the scale of its work into rebuilt and modernised premises, while never ceasing to provide the home nursing services for which it was first established.

Getting From Here to There

THE TURNPIKE ROADS

The local roads were managed by the parish vestries, and paid for out of highway rates. In the early eighteenth century men who could not afford the rate still sometimes offered their labour instead. As well as maintenance, there was the problem of preventing obstructions on the highway. Builders such as William Rhodes thought little of blocking up established footpaths, brickmakers' carts churned up side roads, and the calico printers of Upper Clapton installed a large dog to deter legitimate strollers along the paths across their drying grounds.

The main roads were gradually handed over to turnpike trustees, who administered a system of tolls borne by local residents and travellers from further afield alike. The tolls varied according to the number of horses drawing a vehicle, or the number of wheels it had. When the tolls were last fixed, in 1829, the toll for a single horse was a penny in winter and a penny halfpenny in summer.

The turnpike trustees also took over responsibility both for lighting and for providing watchmen along the main thoroughfares, although there were often complaints that they neglected to do so. They also had to be vigilant to prevent the evasion of tolls. As secondary roads, such as Navarino and Graham Roads, were developed, their entrances were barred by side gates to stop them becoming alternatives to the high road. But the parish authorities refused to take responsibility for the new roads created to serve building development until they had been properly made up, which was often the builder's last priority and sometimes was left until he had become insolvent.

Traffic may have been slower and sparser, but reckless and daredevil driving, often the cause of fatality, found its place in newspaper reports. And traffic grew. By 1861 the police were invoked to assist the Turnpike Commissioners in clearing a 200-yard stretch of the Hackney Road of costers'

105. Clapton toll, at the junction with Lea Bridge Road. From an oil painting by Pollard, c1830.

carts to allow the passage of traffic.

By this date the turnpike system had had its day. The main roads were handed over to commissioners to manage London roads generally in 1826, and all the roads in their turn had been returned to parish authorities in 1863. By then they were better equipped to tackle such work since the creation of municipal vestries and boards of work in 1855. Gradually the tollhouses disappeared, that at Clapton in 1856, several others in 1864, the toll on Lea Bridge Road not until 1872.

A special toll, until it too was abolished in 1872, was payable for use of the Lea Bridge. This bridge had been built in 1757 at a point, called Jeremy's Ferry, at which the river had traditionally been crossed by boat. The associated development of Lea Bridge Road was seen at the time as a logical extension through Epping Forest of the New Road from Paddington to Islington now known as Marylebone, Euston and City Roads. The original wooden bridge over the Lea was replaced by a stone one (illustration 111) in 1820. Another wooden bridge, affording access from Homerton to Temple Mills, collapsed in 1803 while a wagon and two horses were passing over it, and for long afterwards it was repaired only for pedestrian use, being eventually reconstructed in 1882.

106. Kingsland tollhouse, from Ball's Pond Road, 1852.

THE LEA RIVER

The river itself (called the Lee by Parliament, and the Lea by almost everyone else) was an economical alternative to the toll roads, especially for moving heavy loads such as those going to and from the East London breweries. The navigation (originally claimed by the City Corporation, and controlled by Commissioners from the fifteenth century) was improved by cuts approved by statute in 1570, in 1769 and again in 1850. It was ultimately linked via the Hertford Union Canal – a disastrous speculation by Sir George Duckett – to the Regent's Canal, opened in 1820.

HORSE POWER

Traffic congestion in central Hackney led in 1769 to the establishment of coach-stands with seven places in the Narroway, and a further thirteen in what is now Lower Clapton Road. Until the bridge over the Brook was built in 1799, wet weather in the winter months generally led to flooding of the stream, and coachmen demanding higher fares for fording it. Other routes remained impassable, however. The minister at the Gravel Pit meeting place in Chatham Place had to go all the way round

107. *Lea Bridge tollhouse, c1900.*

108. *The Regent's Canal, opened in 1820, provided an economical alternative to the turnpike roads for bulky cargoes. This view shows the canal at Balmes.*

109. A Clapton horse bus passing St Thomas's Square, painted by Pollard c1830.

by the Churchwell path from his home in Cassland Road to take a service when the brook was in flood. In such years the marsh-dwellers were driven to the upper floors of their houses.

Matthews's watercolour of 1852 (illustration 110) of Kingsland Road and its surviving Georgian crescent, shows a remarkable range of the wheeled vehicles still to be seen on Hackney roads, though the North London Railway had cut the services of stage coaches. The coach drivers were notorious for their love of speed. A family returning to Bishopsgate from an outing to Hackney in 1761 were severely injured when the stage coach drivers taking them began to race each other, and the following year saw two fatal accidents from the same cause.

James Pollard's painting (illustration 109) shows one of the horse-drawn buses that had been plying between Hackney and the City and West End since the 1820s. Clapton generated the most traffic. Twelve buses departed more than forty times a day

for the Flower-Pot in Bishopsgate, but there were nearly as many daily return journeys performed by Hackney's seven. Most routes lay to the City, but it was also possible to travel from Clapton via Islington to Oxford Street, and from Stoke Newington to the West End or to Fleet Street. By the 1830s competition between rival bus proprietors was so fierce that there were prosecutions for 'furious driving' along straight stretches such as Hackney Road.

Many of the independent bus operators were bought out in 1855-6 by the London and General Omnibus Company. By this time there was also a route from Kingsland to the Elephant and Castle. The Kingsland Road in particular was one of London's busiest, and here especially competition from independent operators continued. With the growth in the local population from the mid-1840s, by 1859 the Turnpike Commissioners estimated that there were 390 omnibus journeys each day between Shoreditch Church and the turnpike at

Cambridge Heath.

In the mid-1840s the main roads through Hackney, such as Cambridge Heath Road and Kingsland Road, had been paved with flagstones and raised kerbs, and some of them widened. But they remained very dusty since they were watered infrequently by the parish water cart: eventually metalling the road surface put an end to the dust.

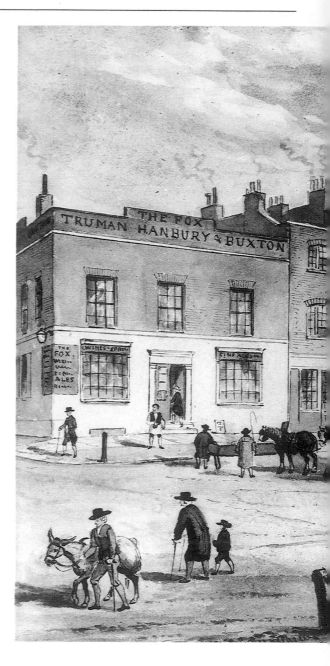

110. *Kingsland Road in 1852, looking south from the corner of Middleton Road towards Kingsland Crescent. Watercolour, 1852, by C.H. Matthews. Note the original building of the Fox pub on the left; the first licensee, Edward Fox, opened for business here in 1727.*

111. *The new Lea Bridge, built in 1820.*

112. *Storer's forge on the south side of Stoke Newington Church Street, demolished in 1870.*

113. Mare Street in 1853.

THE COMING OF THE TRAINS

Trains came to Hackney in 1850, in the form of the clumsily named East & West India Docks & Birmingham Junction Railway. In its early years this line was, not altogether surprisingly, known as the 'Camden Town Railway', as not only was its full title a mouthful but its primary purpose was to link the London & North Western Railway's goods junction at Camden Town with the London docks. But it was soon successful for passenger traffic also, via its link with the Eastern Counties Railway, and in 1853 became officially the North London Railway.

A journalist's account of the delights of a journey on the line in 1851 mentions the 'verdant fields' between the marshes and the 'retired village' of Homerton, but has nothing to say about the crass impact of the railway bridge as it crosses the ancient village centre of Hackney, within a few yards of St Augustine's church tower. The original station was on the east side of the street, above Bohemia Place.

During the first fifteen years passengers from Camden and Islington, as well as Hackney, reached the City (Fenchurch Street) by a circuitous route through Bow. Then, in association with the LNWR,

whose north-westerly lines were generating enormous traffic for the service, the line from Kingsland down to Broad Street was constructed, and opened in 1865. The first station at Victoria Park was opened in 1856, at the suggestion of Sir John Cass's charity estate, which was trying to develop its land on the north side of the park for housing; this station also was later re-sited. By 1854 the North London was already connected to the Great Eastern at Stratford from this junction. The station at Homerton was not opened until 1868. By this time the idea of 'workmen's trains', offering rock-bottom fares to labourers and other low wage-earners, had taken hold, and the parliamentary authorisation for the Broad Street line was one of the first which required a provision of one such train a day for the fare of a penny.

One of the earliest, and most publicly alarming, railway murders took place on the North London, not long before it was re-routed through Dalston, when a bank clerk on his way back from Lombard Street failed to reach his Hackney home. His body was thrown from the train, his pockets plundered, near the canal at Wick Lane. His murderer, one Muller, was arrested in New York by police who intercepted his ship by taking a steamer. Following this incident observation windows were introduced into railway compartments as a reassurance to passengers, and came to be known as 'Muller's lights'.

The workmen's trains did not themselves have a noticeable impact on Hackney's development, and despite its effect on Mare Street the North London had come sufficiently early for the area, by and large, to adapt itself round the railway. It was otherwise with the Great Eastern Railway's line to Enfield, planned from the early days of the company in 1862, although not built until 1869-70. While bringing swift communication with the City to Stoke Newington once Liverpool Street opened in 1874, the line brought blight to the area closer to London. It dominated the west side of Hackney Downs, ploughed straight across Stoke Newington Common, and brought in its wake not only the creeping railwayside industrialisation that killed off the east side of London Fields as a pleasant residential area, but also pockets of poor and jerry-built housing. Notably this included the so-called 'Navvie's Island', which housed the builders of the railway themselves, in a group of

114. The North London Railway and the watercress plantation, 1851.

115. Victoria Park station, c1905.

streets formed in 1869 on a triangle of land enclosed by the railway and the backs of houses west of Rendlesham Road.

MORE WHEELS ON RAILS

In 1870 new competition for the railways, in the form of the horse-drawn trams of the North Metropolitan Tramways Company, appeared. The great advantage of the trams was that the smooth tracking enabled a carriage with fifty passengers to be pulled by the same two horses needed for the traditional bus, which had a maximum payload of twenty-six. After swift development in Whitechapel the company expanded its operation extensively into Islington and Hackney, as well as further east, between 1871 and 1875. The tram network branched from the Angel to Shoreditch church, and via Ball's Pond Road to Kingsland. By 1875 trams ran from Finsbury via Newington Green to Clissold Park; up Kingsland Road to Stoke Newington; and from Mile End Gate through Hackney and Clapton to Stamford Hill. An early

line through Bow to Victoria Park was rapidly abandoned, and then, at the very end of the decade, resumed and extended as far as Cassland Road. Like most of the others, this last can be seen as the ancestor of a still-extant bus route.

Further out, there was a short-lived experiment with steam trams, which ran for the latter part of the 1880s from Stamford Hill to Finsbury Park, Ponder's End and Wood Green; but when the North Metropolitan took them over in 1891 horses were re-introduced. In 1892, a separate company opened a line which joined Clapton with Leyton and beyond, across the Lea Bridge. By the early 1900s, it was clear that the era of electricity had arrived. Electrification of the main routes throughout Hackney began in 1907, and was virtually complete by 1913. At the same time, of course, the trams' own ultimate nemesis had arrived in the form of the motor bus, which superseded the horse bus completely during the years between 1906 and 1911. But the horses were not pensioned off entirely until the tramway from South Hackney through Victoria Park was electrified in 1921.

116. Horse tram at Upper Clapton, photographed by Alfred Braddock c1890.

117.   *Steam tram at Stamford Hill, c1880.*

118.   *Electric trams, Stoke Newington High Street, c1910.*

The Developing Suburbs

THE EARLY ESTATES

Before the mid-nineteenth century, systematic house-building in Hackney and Stoke Newington was on a limited scale. The developments of the eighteenth and early nineteenth centuries, even those by the largest landowners, had been of villas built in ones and twos, or of terraces rarely more than twenty houses long. Small though some of the developments were, Hackney and Stoke Newington are, however, almost entirely the creation of the speculative builder.

Lamb's Farm, with a large acreage at Dalston, was developed from the second decade of the nineteenth century by the astute and unscrupulous William Rhodes (grandfather of Cecil); and although large-scale building here did not start until the 1840s, Rhodes, some twenty years earlier, was boldly building around the fringe of London

Fields on what was then believed to be common land. The neighbouring estate to the south was the property of Sir William Middleton. Although not fully developed until the 1860s, the part at the west end of Middleton Road, and around Albion Square, was built from 1840 under the supervision of George Pownall.

In 1821, the largest farm in Stoke Newington parish, which lay between Church Street and Newington Green and contained some sixty acres, came up for sale. About a quarter of this was acquired by Thomas Cubitt, then at the beginning of his outstanding career as builder and developer. During the 1820s he built up the northern end of Albion Road, either by deploying his own workforce or by letting the land to other builders. But demand was not substantial until the early 1830s, when much of the ground was still in use as market gardens. Altogether, Cubitt's Albion Road property took over twenty years to develop fully for housing. Partly, no doubt, this was because Cubitt insisted on a substantial style of house likely to let – as let it did – to City business and professional families.

119. St John's Terrace, Lauriston Road, built 1843-4. Nos 50-54 survive. The developer was a City cooper, John Parr, and the architect his son, Samuel.

ST JOHN'S TERRACE.

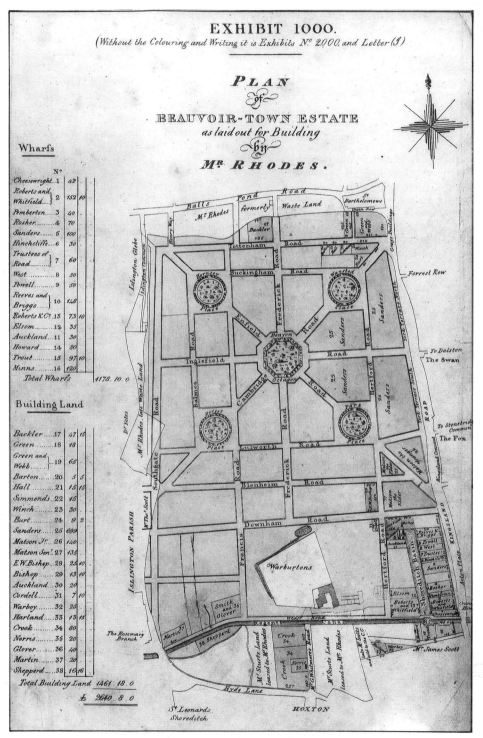

120. *The De Beauvoir estate as Rhodes planned to develop it, c1825.*

THE DE BEAUVOIR ESTATE

Much larger was the Balmes estate, bought from the Whitmores in 1680 by the de Beauvoir family, whose heir, a Tyssen descendant called Benyon, assumed the de Beauvoir name. Early in the nineteenth century, following an approach by Rhodes, the estate was let for building by its then owner, the frail and elderly Reverend Peter de Beauvoir, and an elaborate road scheme was devised, with a central octagon leading to four satellite squares. But building had barely begun when the Rev. de Beauvoir's heir challenged the deal in court. Rhodes and his associates, the Tebbutts, father and son, solicitors of low repute who were acting for both sides, failed to impress the jury. The lease was found to have been unfairly obtained, and in 1834 the de Beauvoirs regained their land, and set about developing it fully and swiftly by leasing to a variety of builders and developers. De Beauvoir Town, attractive to a growing middle class on account not only of its solid and low-density building but its accessibility to the City, was complete by the early 1840s, though only part of the original layout, including the south-eastern square, was realised. The surviving houses of De Beauvoir Square represent the estate's most distinctive architecture.

OTHER ESTATES

The 1840s also saw systematic development on the Rhodes estate – much denser than on the de Beauvoir land – and also on the South Hackney estates belonging to St Thomas's Hospital (around King Edward's Road) and on those of the Sir John Cass' Charity (around Well Street Common). Here and elsewhere estate owners' plans were only partly realised when the recession of the mid-1850s struck, and house-building slowed down considerably. Building on the latter two estates, as with the area north of Shacklewell, was completed only in the 1870s, and, as in Stoke Newington, substantial detached villas became less common than smaller houses built in terraces. The usual method was for the estate owner to enter into an agreement with a builder or developer, commonly for a small number of houses at a time but sometimes for as many as 150, and for the builder to be granted a lease of the 'improved' land once the buildings had been roofed in.

121. Culford Road, c1905, looking north and east from Northchurch Road.

LAND SOCIETIES

In the mid-1850s freehold land societies began to make their mark on London. These were founded as a political manoeuvre to enable more men to qualify to vote in Parliamentary elections – despite the extension of the franchise in 1832, ownership of property was still essential. The earliest society to acquire land in the area was the National Freehold Land Society, which laid out the roads (named after poets) in Stoke Newington's Albert Town from 1852 to 1855. Thus the parts of Stoke Newington that were developed earliest were the two large areas – Albert Town and the Palatine estate – which formed part of the detached South Hornsey parish. There were also at least two freehold land societies operating in Hackney: one (like the National Society) for the Whig interest, which built Warneford and Fremont Streets from 1854 onwards, and one for the Conservatives, which built on land straddling Urswick Road. This estate was laid out for building from St John's Church Road to Templar Road by 1860, although, like its Whig counterpart, it was affected by the building recession and was built up only gradually over twenty years.

The system of building from money raised from weekly subscriptions, adopted by the freehold land societies, was also the mainstay of the mutual benefit building societies which were beginning to provide more of the financial underpinning for builders both large and small. A similar structure underlay the slightly mysterious society which laid out and began to build in Brookfield Road in 1855. Called the Suburban Villa and Village Association, it claimed the *imprimatur* of no less than Lord Shaftesbury. But its first pleasant and spacious villas were probably in the wrong place at the wrong time, and subscriptions faltered.

The London and Suburban Land Company had acquired the Priory, or Clapton Park, estate by 1867, and developed it over the next twenty years. Part of the grounds of the London Orphan Asylum were added on the Asylum's move to Watford. The southern part of the Clapton Park development suffered from the advent of the fever hospital, with some justice, as Dr Tripe, the medical officer of health, was able to demonstrate. The eastern part suffered from the equally justified reputation of being built on tipped household refuse, and the contents of a disused burial ground.

Small scale building, on the other hand, was no guarantee of a good standard. Illustration 122

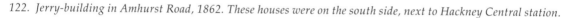

122. Jerry-building in Amhurst Road, 1862. These houses were on the south side, next to Hackney Central station.

W.TELBIN -EVANS SHIRLEY BROOKS Mr.LEMONJun W.JONES F.EVANS MARCUS STONE F.BERGER MARK LEMON AugEGG
  ALBERT SMITH G.C.STANFIELD MISS EVANS -PIGOTT Mrs FRANCIS -LUARD
-KEITH CHAS DICKENS Jun KATE DICKENS MISS HOGARTH MARY DICKENS WILKIE COLLINS MISS H.HOGARTH
  CHARLES DICKENS COPYRIGHT

123. Dickens, Wilkie Collins and other writers and entertainers in the garden of F.M. Evans, proprietor of Punch, in Church Row, Stoke Newington Church Street. A photograph taken before 1860.

depicts the terrace, the work of one Amos, on the south side of Amhurst Road next to the station, after its collapse, part-built, in 1862. Jerry-building became a hot topic of the time.

There is scarcely an undeveloped site on the 1870 Ordnance Survey map of Dalston, and the unbuilt tracts to the east, in central Hackney and Lower Clapton, are largely accounted for by Clapton Park. It was now Stoke Newington's turn. A number of estates were enfranchised, or put on the market, in the early 1870s, and for the first time there was extensive building beyond the ribbon developments along the ancient main thoroughfares. The journalist and pioneer of suburban gardening, Shirley Hibberd, had moved to Lordship Terrace in the 1850s, when, tellingly, it was known as Meadow Street. A few years later he was to note that although nightingales could still be heard, 'all around the builders are drawing a close cordon of bricks'. Wealthy and professional Hackney had gained a substantial influx of clerks, small tradesmen and skilled artisans in the 1860s. But Stoke Newington remained the preserve of the wealthy for rather longer, the principal development at this

time being on the Church Commissioner's estate between Lordship Park and the reservoir. Church Street was still a good address (illustration 123), but south of it, the 1870s and early 80s saw the most dramatic growth, in smaller, less expensive houses, echoing the trend in Hackney in the previous decade.

In both parishes most development was of houses intended for single family occupation, and for the most part they were so occupied. Although subdivision was far from unknown, this tended to occur in larger, older houses, particularly in those which had reached the end of their building lease lives.

MODEL DWELLINGS FOR THE WORKING CLASSES

There was relatively little building of flats, although some went up in Graham Road (much less elaborate than the original design) and in lower Clapton, including those in Clapton Square and, notably, Rowhill Road. Unique flats were built around gardens in Manor Road and Bethune Road by Matthew Allen, in 1873-5. In addition to this middle-class development, Allen worked with Sir Sydney Waterlow's Improved Industrial Dwellings Company, for whom he designed innumerable blocks of dwellings for respectable artisans in different parts of central London.

The 'model dwellings' movement, for improvement in standards of working-class housing, made less impact in Hackney and Stoke Newington than in the crowded central areas or even in Islington. But, under the aegis of the Metropolitan Association for Improving the Dwellings of the Industrious Classes, it did create Gibson Buildings (now Gardens), a mix of flats and cottages, in Northwold Road in 1892. The present owners of the estate have seen fit to obliterate the original entablature *(illustration 125)*. Other developments in the same tradition were Coronation and Imperial Avenues, in 1902-3, west of the high road through Stoke Newington, built by the Four Per Cent Industrial Dwellings Company. This company was founded in 1885, principally to relieve the appalling conditions of the Jewish poor in the East End and Spitalfields, and its name derives from its stated intention to give investors a four per cent return on their money. Although flats on this first estate were hard to let in the early years the company went on to build Navarino Mansions, and a further 300 flats in similar parallel blocks, off Ralston Lane, which were completed in 1905. The contractor for Gibson Gardens was John Grover, who had a large depot on the New North Road. On his own account he redeveloped the site of the old Shacklewell manor house, to form April, Seal and Perch Streets. These buildings, from 1881 onwards, were constructed to look like cottages, but each front door originally led to two flats, a building type which became popular later, especially at Upper Clapton. Other privately constructed flats include Great Eastern Buildings in Reading Lane, built by Mowlems in 1892, and Sylvester House, promoted by the neighbouring clothing manufacturers, Stapley and Smith, in 1909.

124. *Plans and elevations for 'middle-class' flats in Graham Road, a project of 1892 which did not proceed. Graham Mansions, a somewhat less opulent project designed by Ernest Schreider, were built in 1896.*

125. *Gibson Gardens (originally Gibson Buildings) in 1966. Photo by Frank Chambers.*

The Traders

SMALL BEGINNINGS

When the nineteenth century opened Hackney was still a large village, and its shops village shops. The new bourgeoisie who had moved in to Hackney Grove or Lower Clapton Road would use Church Street – as the narrow part of Mare Street was called – for fresh produce. Fruit and vegetables, dairy and meat products would be from local gardeners, cowkeepers and butchers, and there were many pubs which brewed their own beer. But for most clothing, and household goods other than the most basic, they would look to the Hackney Road, Shoreditch or the City.

The parish census of 1821, the middle one of a series of three decennial censuses for Hackney parish which to our great good fortune have survived, shows that Church Street was beginning by this date to have more sophisticated shops. Today, indeed, we may envy Church Street's china shops, toy shop and bookshop of this time. All of these, as it happens, were run by women, as was the circulating library at Kingsland.

By mid-century all had changed. The growth in population, the creation of canal and railway, brought both the demand and the ability to satisfy it. By 1853, when the lithograph of Church Street (illustration 126) was made, it and its rival, Kingsland Road, had become sophisticated and fashionable shopping streets. The transformation from small-time village trader to confident late Victorian merchant is personified in Matthew Rose, a draper, whose business moved in 1868 from old-fashioned premises to a grand new store on the site now occupied by Marks and Spencer; here it flourished until 1936.

Away from the hub of Hackney a number of other shopping centres grew up. One of the busiest was Well Street, where among the trades not so readily found in the area today there were active in 1869 a music seller, a tinman, oil and colour retailers, a dyer, a harness maker and a corn dealer, portmanteau makers, gas-fitters, pawnbrokers, a blind-maker, and several marine stores. For refreshment, there were coffee and dining-rooms, and an eel and pie house.

126. *Mare Street, looking south along the Narroway. A lithograph of 1853.*

127. Matthew Rose's first shop in Mare Street, c1850.

128. Matthew Rose's new store. This lithograph of 1868 comes from an advertisement which drew attention to the Amhurst Road entrance being more convenient for carriages than that in Mare Street.

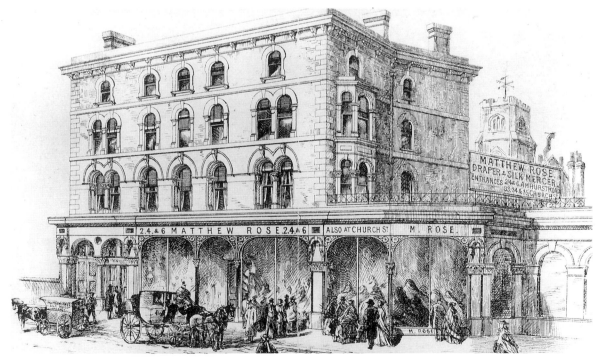

THE WIFE'S ADVISER

SHOULD be read by every Married Woman as it contains Sixty pages of plain and practical advice, necessary to be known to Ladies. Specimen Copy will be sent free, on receipt of two stamps for postage, or the same bound in cloth, eight stamps. Illustrated Lists, post free.

E. LAMBERT & SON,

Manufacturers of Surgical Appliances, Accouchement and Nursing Requisites

60 & 62, QUEEN'S RD., DALSTON, LONDON N.E.

Wear DUNN'S FAMOUS HATS

3/9
All One Price!

THE 1900
Largest Sale in the World.   50 Branches.

D'EPOTS:
535, Kingsland Road.
173, High Street, Stoke Newington.

Write for an Estimate.

GOODS WAREHOUSED
FLOOD & SON
219 QUEEN'S RD., DALSTON, LONDON.
ESTABLISHED 1840.
ESTIMATES FREE

PANTECHNICON VANS by the hour or contract.

THE SPEAKER'S CACHOU

In Packets,
1 d.

For SMOKERS and SINGERS

Sold Everywhere by
Chemists and Confectioners.

WALKER'S ARTIFICIAL TEETH DEPÔT

For High-Class Work at Strictly Moderate Charges.

Sets Complete from One Guinea.
Painless Stoppings and Extractions, 2/6.

Principal—
H. E. WALKER, 5, High Street, Kingsland.
(2 minutes from this Theatre).
Advice Free, 9 till 8; Thursdays, 6.

Teeth Under this Size Extracted

AT **6 D.**   EACH

SUNDAYS—ONE SHILLING.

NORFOLK'S DRUG STORES,   19, BALLS POND RD., LONDON, N.

Allen Bros.' Footballs

Boxing Gloves.

Dumb Bell.

Bar Bells.

RUGBY

Boxing Gloves.

Indian Clubs.

Fencing Sticks.

ALL WINTER SPORTS AND GAMES.
Air Guns and Pistols, Saloon Rifles and Ammunition.

496, KINGSLAND ROAD (near Forest Rd.)

Madame O. GROSSE,

Practical Corset Maker.
RENOWNED FOR STYLE, FIT, AND QUALITY.

Corsets Made to Measure.
Largest Stock in London.

494 KINGSLAND ROAD, N.E.,
78 HIGH ST., STOKE NEWINGTON, N.,
24 EAST ROAD, CITY ROAD.
Established Over 20 Years.

129. *Miscellaneous advertisements from 1900.*

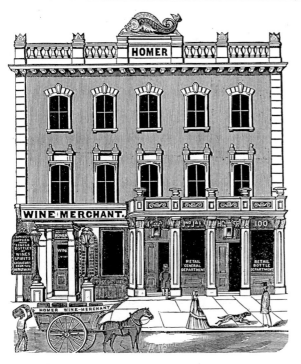

130. The Dolphin, Mare Street, owned by J. J. Homer (developer of Homer Road). A woodcut, c 1860.

THE MARKETS

The street markets probably originated with the costermongers who would congregate wherever shoppers shopped. Unauthorised, and often obstructive to road traffic, the markets were tolerated because they offered a genuine opportunity to retail surplus goods to the consumer at rock-bottom prices. Sometimes the stall-holders found opposition from local shopkeepers; sometimes the shopkeepers joined in by setting up stalls themselves.

Most of today's street markets began in the 1880s. The oldest, and largest, originally with some forty stalls, was in Chatsworth Road, where the wide street afforded minimum obstruction to traffic. Well Street market, established about 1886, has moved from selling mostly perishables to other kinds of merchandise. Ridley Road market, the liveliest of all, is not recorded as early as the others, and may well have resulted from unsatisfied demand when a market at Kingsland High Street was, at official insistence, relocated further south in the interests of free traffic flow, and thus amalgamated with a smaller market, now enlarged and still flourishing, held between Ralston Lane and Forest Road.

THE LONG ESTABLISHED

Many individual businesses were as resilient as the markets. Amongst those that passed their centenary were the undertakers, Hawes of Well Street, and the estate agents Bunch and Duke, of Mare Street. E. Gibbons, the furniture store which closed in 2002, calculated their history from their foundation as a rag merchant's business by Thomas Gibbons in Morning Lane, though the real driving force was his daughter Elizabeth, who took her wardrobe and furniture business from Brett Road to one of the sixfold premises in Amhurst Road about 1898. Fish Brothers, the jewellers, descend from a business first found in local directories in 1872, when W. G. Fish had premises both in Mare Street (opposite the present shop) and in Kingsland High Street. In Stoke Newington, in particular, builders' merchants had remarkable longevity, particularly Smith and Sons, established in Mathias Road by 1876, and, in Church Street, Whincop's, established as a gas fitter's business in the 1840s. One of the best known of Hackney's old-established businesses, F. Cooke, purveyors of eels to Kingsland High Street (and well beyond) closed in 1996, though the splendid early 20th century decor of their premises has been preserved for the benefit of the customers of their Chinese successors.

But for sheer staying power nothing comes close to the pubs. Though these rarely tended to stay in a family for more than two generations, it is commonplace for a sign to persist, indeed a handful can be traced for almost three centuries on the same site. Though all have been rebuilt, sometimes more than once, a few which survived at least until the late 20th century can be traced back to 1730 or beyond. Notable survivors (sometimes under other, transient names) are the Plough at Homerton, the Cat and Mutton on London Fields, the White Hart at Clapton, the Three Crowns and the Rochester Castle at Stoke Newington and the Cock and the Horse and Groom in Mare Street. The Rose and Crown at Cambridge Heath has closed, and the Robin Hood at Upper Clapton been demolished. The Jolly Butchers in Stoke Newington High Street dates from the mid-eighteenth century, the Fox in Kingsland Road from the 1780s. From the 1820s onwards there were many more, and only the recent fashion for reinventing traditional establishments for specialised markets, or converting them to other uses, disguises many of the alehouses which were thoughtfully provided with the suburban housing developments of the mid to late 19th century.

131. *G.J. Wood's outfitters in Kingsland Road.*

132. *A page from the catalogue of Wood's the outfitters.*

Schooldays

A PLACE FOR PRIVATE SCHOOLS

From the mid-seventeenth century onwards, fashionable London society sent its children to the numerous boarding schools established in the clean air and rural seclusion of places like Hackney and Stoke Newington. Although it is not known where his premises were, the lexicographer, Robert Ainsworth, moved his Bethnal Green school to Hackney around 1700. An influential writer, who made a comfortable fortune out of schoolmastering, his concept of the ideal school was a large house some way out of London; it would have a roll of no more than twelve children, taught by two masters, one of whom spoke in Latin at all times so that it would be learnt as if it were the children's native tongue. (Later in the century the French Academy in Well Street offered language tuition on the same principle.) Another seemingly very modern feature of Ainsworth's thinking was his abhorrence of punishments of all kinds; he believed in motivation only through rewards.

Hackney's most prestigious school in the eighteenth century was Dr Newcome's Academy, also known merely as Hackney School. When it closed in 1819, it had flourished for over a century (the site was taken by the London Orphan Asylum). The annual play, perhaps a piece from the classics or from Shakespeare, became a fashionable court event. The presentation in 1770, *Macbeth*, was, in true theatrical tradition, postponed by the illness of members of the cast.

As the wealthier inhabitants of Hackney gave up their large old houses to move elsewhere, so suitable premises were left vacant for schools and private asylums. Clapton House, at Clapton Pond, the residence formerly of both Bishop Wood and of the Powells, became a school, as did the old family home of Sir John Cass in South Hackney, and another large house on the present site of Meynell Gardens. A girls' school existed in Fleetwood House, in Stoke Newington Church Street, for more than fifty years from the 1770s; Sutton House, divided in two, saw more than one school come and go. Many smaller premises, including modest town houses in Clapton Square, Cassland Road and Stoke Newington Church Street, were found suitably flexible for instruction of both boarding and day pupils.

Throughout the eighteenth and nineteenth centuries the local private schools competed fiercely

133. Clapton House School (on the present site of Thistlewaite Road), c1860. The novelist Anthony Hope, whose father was headmaster, was born here in 1863.

134. *Dr Newcome's Academy, seen about 1815. A lithograph by Reeves. The school was situated in about 8 acres; between 70 and 80 boys were accommodated in the large gabled building, supervised by a resident usher.*

for the attention of upwardly mobile parents. Mrs Larkham of Dalston ('a pleasant and healthful village' in 1791, according to her advertisements) emphasised that her clientele were from 'the families of the highest Respectability'. The pompous brochure of Wick Hall School in the 1840s made much not only of the healthfulness of Hackney Wick and of the pupils' diet (which included 'the beautiful milk of several fine cows') but of its proximity to the 'Royal' Victoria Park. The Misses Rutherfoord of Upper Clapton found it worthwhile to advertise their school for young ladies as far afield as the West Indies, where much Lower Clapton money was made.

Both young ladies and gentlemen could expect to be taught English language, composition, history, geography, writing, arithmetic, drawing and dancing. Fencing might be offered to boys, and French, Italian and occasionally Latin, to both boys and girls, often as an optional extra. Activities usually on offer which do not find a special place in the modern curriculum were instruction in 'the use of the globes', and 'military marching' for boys, the latter surviving as 'drill' as a standard feature in schools well into the 20th century.

THE CHARITY SCHOOLS

Provision for the education of local children, however, is recorded much earlier than any of the schools with social aspirations. By 1616 there were two small schools, one endowed by a bequest to the Skinners' Company, housed in 'Urswick's House', the Church House, in Hackney churchyard. In 1714 they were absorbed into a charity school founded for poor parishioners' children. Here thirty boys and twenty girls were, like the pupils of many similar institutions, expected to wear a distinctive uniform. Another parish charity, the 'School of Industry', ultimately housed in Dalston Lane until its closure in the 1890s, gave poor children a practical training in manual work.

Hackney Parochial School moved from the churchyard to Plough Lane in Homerton, and then in 1811 to newly-built premises in Chatham Place *(illustration 136)*; later it added a former Board school in Wilton Road and the site of Ram's school in Urswick Road to its sites. Now it is unified on the Paragon Road site in a new building. South and West Hackney each had its own parish school: the latter's building still stands *(illustration 137)*. Many of the non-conformist sects which abounded in the area, from the Presbyterians of St Thomas's Square to the Quakers of Lordship Road, had

135. Wick Hall School, c1845. Its site is now Chapman Road.

established their own schools to ensure instruction in their own religious beliefs.

In 1784 the Stoke Newington vestry, which had previously paid local people to teach children in their own homes, established a charity school, which later came under the umbrella of the church school movement as St Mary's Parochial School; another church school, St Matthias's, was founded in 1849. Stoke Newington also had a 'ragged school' founded about 1842, in a 'rookery', Lawrence's Buildings, near Newington Common, for children without hope of any other schooling. Its managers had persistent trouble finding suitable teachers because of 'the violence and rudeness of the children'. The school's committee evidently regarded it as a major triumph if a child could be induced to transfer to St Mary's or St Matthias's, or if a former pupil managed to hold down a 'respectable situation' for a few months. Lawrence's Buildings were eventually redeveloped at the insistence of Hackney's energetic medical officer of health, Dr J.W. Tripe, and new tenements were built on the site.

THE RIVALS

It was 1829 before the middle-class inhabitants of Hackney founded a school for their own sons. This was the Grammar School in Sutton Place, which, although required to have an Anglican clergyman as headmaster, attracted pupils from all denominations. Its exclusivity was social: no shopkeeper in Hackney could, in practice, have his son admitted. It is scarcely surprising that the rival Church of England School, founded the fol-

lowing year in Clarence Road not only to provide for the shopkeepers excluded by the Grammar School, but in a ferment of anti-secularism associated with the contemporary foundation of King's College in the Strand, was ultimately more successful. To the boys at least, however, class proved a unifying force. A long-running feud between the two schools ended when some small boys from Sutton Place were bullied by boys from the Parochial School: incensed by the presumption of the 'charity brats', the Clarence Road school-boys joined the fray on behalf of their middle-class fellows. Indeed such was the behaviour of Hackney's future leaders that the police had to be called before order could be restored.

Even denominational education was unashamedly a matter of class, often signified merely by the level of the fees. At Dalston, in the 1880s, middle-class Methodists would presumably expect to send their children to the Dalston Wesleyan Middle Class School in Lenthall Road, and to pay up to a shilling (5p) per week.

BOARD SCHOOLS BEGIN

With the foundation of the London School Board in 1870 there began a revolution in education: it became compulsory to the age of 12, had to be provided systematically, and hence could not be left to the market. The Board took over many existing schools, several of them denominational, and set out to remedy the shortfall of elementary school places needed over and above those already provided by the independent schools which the Board considered 'efficient'. To meet both existing

136. Hackney charity school, on the east side of Chatham Place just south of Paragon Road; as it appeared c.1820.

137. *The girls of West Hackney Church Schools in 1864. The building (of 1838) still stands in Evering Road.*

138. *Hackney Grammar School, at the west end of Sutton Place. The building later became a house, Sutton Lodge. Watercolour by Hawkins, 1836.*

deficiency and a growing population, by 1904 there were more than 12,000 new places provided, in twenty-two centres run by the Board in Hackney, and four in Stoke Newington. Several centres provided places for the mentally or physically handicapped, and there were specialist centres offering facilities for cookery, laundry, 'housewifery' and manual training. From 1882 onwards the Board also set out to provide what it called 'continuing education' for anybody over the school-leaving age of 12; most of its centres held 'evening continuation schools'. The Board was proud that it set no upper age limit, and that its oldest scholar had been in his eighties.

The Board's handsome new buildings incensed parsimonious ratepayers such as Hackney's historian Benjamin Clarke, a survivor of the battle of Sutton Place. He was far from untypical amongst the likes of former pupils of Clarence Road in considering that plainer, more humdrum architecture would be quite good enough for the children of those too poor to pay for educating their children themselves.

By the close of the nineteenth century private schools were still flourishing; they still had a monopoly of secondary level education. It had been an avowed aim of the highly successful Grocers' Company School, established on the south side of Hackney Downs in 1876, to serve 'that class who desire to educate their children up to the age of 14 or thereabouts'. Hackney was still apparently a suitable home for a school for middle class girls established by the foundation of Lady Eleanor Holles, whose charity school in Cripplegate had flourished since 1911. In the 1890s it opened the purpose-built Mare Street premises which now house Cordwainer's College. By the 1930s Hackney seemed a less suitable site to its Governors, and the school moved to Hampton.

During the nineteenth century innumerable private schools had come and gone, and by the century's end the emphasis had changed. In Hackney Grove, the Collegiate School for Girls was advertising that its pupils were prepared for employment in Government offices; another girls' school in Kingsland Crescent, established in 1829, had developed along the same lines. The South Hackney College in Ainsworth Road proclaimed that it had not only the practical aim of preparing boys for commercial life, but set out 'to EDUCATE them, to teach them to THINK'.

139. Woodworking at the Hackney Technical Institute, Cassland Road, 1912.

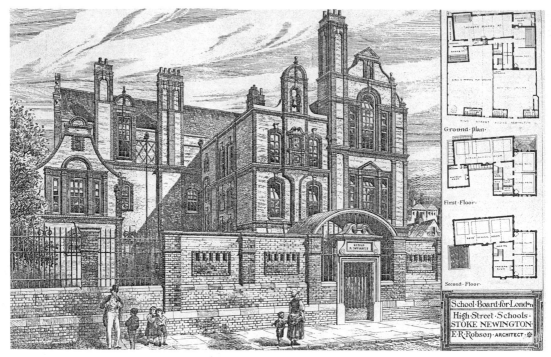

140. The London School Board's school at Stoke Newington High Street (corner of Northwold Road), 1876. The building has been much altered.

141. The Grocers' Company school, during its building in 1875. The school was handed over to the London County Council in 1904 and renamed Hackney Downs School the following year. The building was replaced after a fire in 1963; the school was closed by Government order in 1995.

142. Froggett's Mill at Hackney Wick, about 1840. A site now part of the Trowbridge estate. Samuel Froggett was a spectacle and instrument maker. When he occupied the Mill in the 1820s, it was used in a process for grinding lenses he had first developed in Sheffield.

Work and Play

EARLY FACTORIES

Though industry had long flourished at the Lea Valley mills (Temple Mills in particular being used at various times for the production of gunpowder and the grinding of pins and needles), and land at Spring Hill had been used in calico production, by the beginning of the nineteenth century Hackney had no more than two manufacturing industries. Both were found in the extreme east: the silk mills at Hackney Wick, established on the banks of the Hackney Brook, and Berger's paintworks which, since 1773, had relied on the purity of the water from an artesian well at Homerton while using Hackney Brook to carry effluent away. By the century's close, textile production had long ceased, but a fireworks factory had come and gone in Millfields Road, a rubber works at Lea Bridge had been built over and succeeded by a bottle factory nearby, and on several acres of Hackney Wick, north east of the railway, manufacturers produced tar, varnish, flooring cloth, chemicals and chemical dyes. As ever, the Wick housed the poorest people in the area. The river was heavily polluted, although this

was blamed locally on sewage outfall from Walthamstow and Leyton. There were glue and pencil works at Dalston; Homerton produced parkesine (or xylonite, an early form of cellulose), vinegar and perfume. Particularly in the south, towards Bethnal Green and Shoreditch, small premises manufacturing clothing, furniture and leather goods had proliferated, often in workshops converted from or added on to large houses whose residents had moved further out.

Home-working was common, boxes and leather goods in particular being produced this way. Women did much of this but also, in large numbers, found factory work. In Stoke Newington the population of women still exceeded that of men in 1900, due, perhaps, even then to the presence of a servant population. In Homerton and Hackney Wick the same phenomenon arose because factory work of the type employing men was in decline. Businesses such as Clarnico's sweet factory at the Wick employed mostly girls, as did jam-making, dyeing and cleaning, and parts of the boot-making and tailoring trades.

Clarnico's set out to be a model employer. As well as running a bonus system and giving its women a small 'dowry' on marriage, it ran its own band and choral society.

143. Lea Bridge Mills, Watercolour by Bigot, c1845.

144. *Berger's paintworks, from Morning Lane, in 1910.*

145. *Berger's office and sales staff, photographed at their first staff conference in 1906.*

146. A laundry business existed at 116 Lauriston Road for 75 years from 1899. This picture was taken c1925.

147. *Factory workers at Hackney Wick (Clarnico's factory in the background), drawn by T. Heath Robinson in 1904.*

LOUNGING AT LEISURE

Out of working hours, young families congregated on Hackney Downs; so did courting couples, which enraged the Presbyterian minister at Clapton enough to initiate, in 1911, a newspaper correspondence that accused the police of permitting the Downs to become 'a plague spot ... a cesspool'. Although Charles Booth's *Life and Labour of the London Poor* had made some very similar observations, this view, unsurprisingly, found little public support.

Young single people resorted to Mare Street, and what was famous at the turn of the century as the dismissively-named 'monkey parade' on Sunday evenings. Here, in the last leisure hours of their week, the unattached came to see and be seen. The journalist, George Sims, writing in 1904, was astonished at the women's dress, finding it 'as gay and gorgeous as the costumes that grace the Heath of Hampstead on a Whit Monday', and describing the varieties of bright green, yellow, violet and petunia found in hat, skirt, blouse and waistband as 'absolutely prismatic'. A fine Sunday might mean a trip in a horse-drawn brake to Epping Forest, or boating on the Lea.

148. *Sunday evening in Mare Street, drawn by T. Heath Robinson, 1904*

PARKS FOR THE PEOPLE

Victoria Park, opened in 1845, had its origins in a local campaign. It was to be the first of several. The people of the districts to the south of Hackney were chronically short of open space, and it was apparent to those in the west that the crowded courts of the Tower Hamlets were breeding grounds for contagious diseases that could all too easily spread. The government, under popular pressure, found funds from the sale of the property of the bankrupt Duke of York, and laid out the Park to a design by James Pennethorne. The original plan (illustration 150) was to integrate housing (of a superior quality and intended to help pay for the Park) into the landscaping, in a way reminiscent of the concept of Pennethorne's mentor, John Nash, for Regent's Park. But the housing market was sluggish, and responsibility for the land eventually divided between two sets of government Commissioners. The plans were revised before building started on the north side in 1860, with the result that the house property, both south of Victoria Park Road and north of Approach Road, now seems quite distinct from the open space.

The Park was an instant success, and to the original plan a boating and then a bathing lake were added, the latter hugely popular among young men from the bath-less East End. There were sports pitches, ornamental arches from the old London Bridge, and, on the lake island, a pagoda-style building brought from Hyde Park. Although preaching in the park was banned for a time because of 'unbecoming scenes', the eastern section became a home for soap-box oratory of all kinds, and the natural resort for large-scale meetings and demonstrations, such as during strikes in the docks.

Finsbury Park had a very similar genesis. A meeting in 1850 of residents of Finsbury, who were concerned at the building-over of their local fields round Shepherdess Walk and the Rosemary Branch, resulted in a scheme, again designed by Pennethorne, for 'Albert Park' at Highbury. The plan was aborted by a change of government, and it was not until 1869 that Finsbury Park came into being on a more northerly site, in the grounds of Brownswood manor house and Hornsey Wood Tavern, skirting Hackney's boundary. Amateur gardeners revelled in the floral displays, as they did in Victoria Park, though whereas in the latter there was an enthusiastic bird-watching fraternity, the bird-fanciers of Hornsey and Stamford Hill came equipped with shotguns.

149. Looking at deer in Clissold Park.

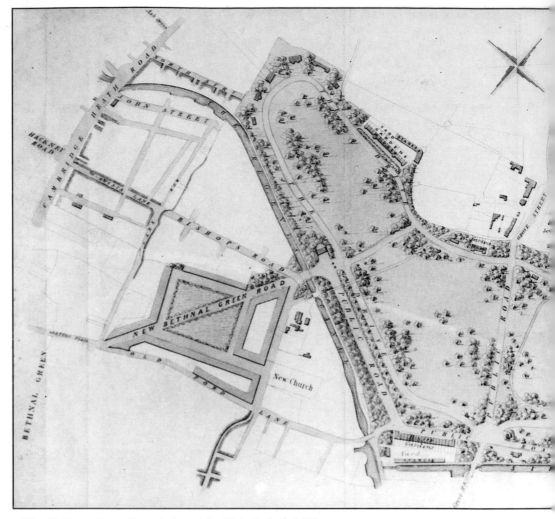

150. Sir James Pennethorne's layout for Victoria Park, 1841.

These parks on the fringes of the area were a splendid bonus for its population, but Hackney retained in its heartland extensive commons, still private property of the lord of the manor subject to lammas and other rights. The 1860s saw the beginnings of the process whereby commons in built-up areas were acquired, under Act of Parliament, for public open spaces. By this time arable farming in Hackney had long been abandoned and even grazing was limited to Mill Fields and the Marshes. Despite the disappearance of the original purpose of common rights, enclosure invariably led to local outrage, as when a builder called Clarkson encroached on London Fields in 1867, or ten years later the Grocers' Company enclosed part of the Downs for the school playground. On London Fields a special hazard was

a particularly boisterous form of rounders, called 'scorchems', played during work-breaks by the young employees of local workshops.

The lord of the manor, now William Amhurst Tyssen-Amherst, later Baron Amherst, drove a hard bargain for his manorial rights, and it was 1884 before Hackney Downs, London Fields, Clapton, Stoke Newington and Well Street Commons became fully the property of the Metropolitan Board of Works.

The Board's successor, the London County Council, formally acquired Clissold Park in 1889, following three 'monster petitions' to save it from building development, and with financial aid from the vestries of Stoke Newington, Hackney, South Hornsey and Islington. Originally called Newington Park when created by Jonathan Hoare,

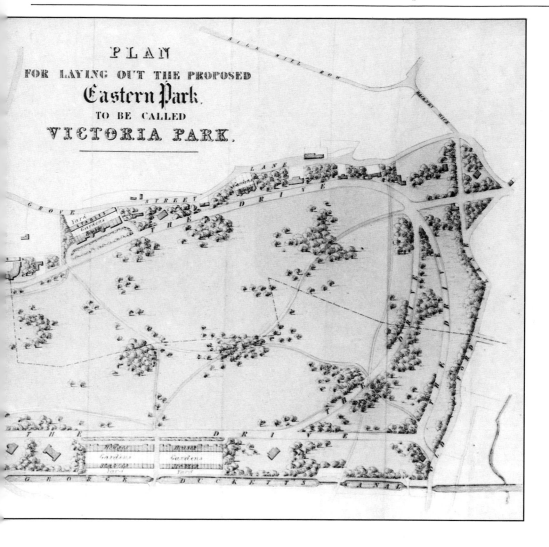

PLAN
FOR LAYING OUT THE PROPOSED
Eastern Park.
TO BE CALLED
VICTORIA PARK.

of the banking family, at the end of the eighteenth century, the landscape of the Park had the advantage, when compared with the bleak ploughed fields from which Finsbury Park was made, of very fine, ancient trees, as well as the presence of the New River. From the beginning, the park managers also encouraged what was then regarded as an innovation, the presence of animals – not sheep grazed by farmers, as happened in Victoria Park well into this century, but guinea pigs, caged birds and deer, donated by members of the public.

It was the young footballers of Hackney Wick who indirectly created the impetus for the acquisition of the Marshes, today still the home of more football pitches than any other open space in London. A chain of events begun by the pastors of the Eton Mission, whose boys' club had had its

goalposts removed by the marsh drivers, led, in 1893, to the acquisition of the Marshes by the LCC. As well as a home for football, the marshes were the haunt of wildfowlers and rabbit-coursers, and home to London's most substantial gipsy population. In flood years, when the ice was thick enough, there was miles of free skating. But the river pollution put an end both to fishing and an open-air bathing pool.

Everyone is likely to have a favourite amongst the glorious group of public parks to which Hackney and Stoke Newington residents have access; the acquisition in 1979 by the borough council of Abney Park Cemetery has afforded another contender, with considerable idiosyncratic appeal, and many smaller open spaces have, through municipal effort, been secured as pleasant

151. Park keepers and constabulary at the opening of Springfield Park in 1905.

green places. A park called Shore Gardens, on a cleared bomb site on Frampton Park Road, earlier formed part of the Loddiges nursery and is to be replanted and renamed in its honour. For many, the jewel in the crown may well be Springfield Park at Upper Clapton, created in 1905 by the merging of the grounds of three substantial villas (only Springfield House surviving), which slope down to Horse Shoe Point and the Lea marshes. Indeed this new park, although more remote than Victoria Park, proved to be a particular draw for special holiday tram excursions for the families of Whitechapel and Spitalfields.

THE LOCAL THEATRES

The earliest major theatre in Hackney opened in the 1860s. Its entrance was off Dalston Lane just east of Dalston Junction station, and in fact it began as the Dalston Circus, becoming successively the North London Colosseum and then, in 1898, after rebuilding, the Dalston Theatre. Part of the shell and the entrance still stand. It was much the largest of the three sizeable theatres in the area, seating three and a half thousand, 500 more than either of its principal rivals. Its staple offerings seem to have been touring productions, running for a week or so on the way in or out of the West End. It was also used for cinema productions from 1912, and by 1922 live performances had ceased. Between the wars it was one of about fifteen cinemas in Hackney, most of which were in and around Mare Street and Kingsland Road.

Quite unexpected, in an otherwise completely residential terraced street, was the 600-seater Theatre Royal, on the north side of Glenarm Road at Lower Clapton. The brainchild of Thomas Turner, a Bethnal Green pharmacy owner, it was built in 1876 behind two houses owned by Turner to the

152. *From a Hackney Empire programme, c1936.*

153. *From a Dalston Theatre programme, 1900.*

designs of the established theatre architect J.T. Robinson. The theatre, also known simply as the Clapton Park Theatre, ran into licensing trouble, on safety grounds, not least because it was estimated (by no less than the London fire chief Captain Shaw) that the premises were some twenty four minutes' travel from the fire station in Bodney Road. After closure in 1884, the damp and dilapidated premises were taken by Thomas Jackson, a Primitive Methodist missionary later well known for his work with destitute boys in Whitechapel. The theatre became the birthplace of the Clapton Park Tabernacle, and the premises at 79-81 Glenarm Road were restored to housing use when the Tabernacle built new premises in Blurton Road. The balconies and balusters of the façade remain as reminders of the theatre (illustration 155).

The Alexandra Theatre in Stoke Newington Road opened in 1897, succumbing in 1906 to the trend away from drama to variety and then to film. Closed during the last war, it remained in business until 1950. The Hackney Empire, on the other hand, which like the Alexandra was designed by Frank Matcham, was intended as a variety theatre from its opening in 1901, achieving great renown in the field, and regularly attracting top performers and appreciative audiences. It was rescued from its post-war incarnation as a bingo club (and from the decapitation of its splendid domes) by teams of imaginative and dedicated enthusiasts, and having transcended a decade of financial uncertainty, continues to flourish.

154. *A scene from Hall Caine's The Christian, presented at the Dalston Theatre at the turn of the century.*

155. *The theatre in Glenarm Road, Lower Clapton, in the 1880s.*

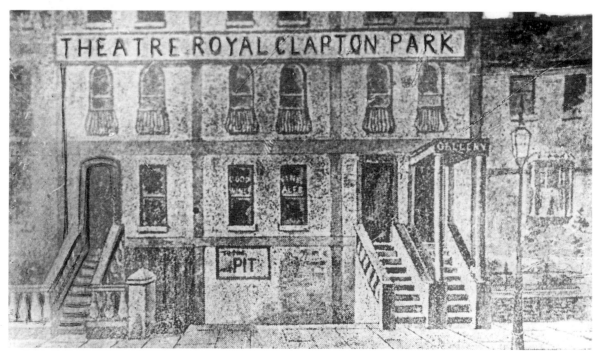

156. *The Alexandra Theatre. From a publicity item at its opening in 1897.*

157. *Views of the Hackney Empire, opened in 1901. Drawn by Frank Matcham.*

158. *A Hackney Empire programme of 1925.*

159. *Horatio Bottomley campaigning in Mare Street, c1920. Bottomley (1860-1933) was an orphan by the time he was five, became an errand boy at fourteen, began a local paper, the Hackney Hansard, when he was 24, and despite an intervening bankruptcy was reportedly a very rich man ten years later. Between 1901-1905 sixty-seven bankruptcy petitions were filed against him. His most famous enterprise was the founding of a jingoist weekly called 'John Bull'. After a colourful life he died in reduced circumstances and obscurity.*

Town Improvements

POLITICAL CHANGES

By the end of the nineteenth century Hackney had lost its radical reputation. Since becoming a separate constituency in 1867 (though joined with parts of Shoreditch and Bethnal Green till 1888, and with Stoke Newington from 1885 till 1918), it sent both Liberal and Conservative members to Parliament. These were of varied distinction and included Henry Fawcett, the blind libertarian politician and reforming Postmaster General, whose interest in Indian matters acquired him the nickname of 'the member for India'; Charles Russell, later Lord Russell of Killowen, a brilliant lawyer, whose popularity reflected strong local commitment to Irish home rule; and Horatio Bottomley, fraudster and self-publicist extraordinary. Bottomley's successor, for Labour, was Herbert Morrison, mayor of Hackney and later Lord Morrison of Lambeth. But on a more local level politics were consistently a matter of keeping down the rates.

Since 1856 Hackney had had an active and vocal medical officer of health. Dr Tripe was the first holder of the office; his role was to oversee the implementation of public health and housing legislation handed down by Parliament. He not only fought a running battle against the unhealthy conditions permitted by landlords in the poorer districts and those where old houses had come to be multi-occupied, but took an important role in campaigns such as that launched by the Victoria Park Preservation Society in 1871, in which it was partially successful in preventing the Crown estate

160. *(above left) A political meeting in Victoria Park, drawn by E.G. Cohen*

161. *(left) Henry Fawcett (1833-84), MP for Hackney from 1874 until his death.*

162. *(above) A postman photographed by St Thomas's church, Clapton Common, c1904.*

163. *The mayor and mayoress of Stoke Newington, Councillor H.J. Beavis and Mrs Beavis, at Alexandra Palace in June 1911 for a children's tea party held to mark the coronation of George V.*

164. The Ladies' Table in the Stoke Newington Reading Room, drawn by Helena Horwitz, 1901.

from completing its scheme to build housing on the north side of the Park. Dr Tripe saw his role as that of waging 'a war of the community against the individual for the public good', but, no doubt pragmatically, he was less persistent when the offending property interest was represented on the vestry, as, unsurprisingly, it often was.

In 1894 Hackney and Stoke Newington's municipal shotgun marriage was dissolved by Act of Parliament. Stoke Newington ran along non-party lines until after 1939 but in Hackney politics grew livelier as the gradual reduction of property qualifications brought a wider spectrum of the population into local government.

LOCAL ENDEAVOURS

Stoke Newington was first to set up a public library, in 1890; later, Passmore Edwards and Carnegie money established and extended permanent premises for it in Church Street. Hackney, like many central areas, showed less enthusiasm, its first library opening in 1908.

Hackney's first baths came in 1897, and Stoke Newington's in 1909. There were major battles over the municipalisation of Hackney's electricity and water; both were achieved, in 1900-2; but before 1919 the major re-housing programmes to replace acknowledged slums, such as the replacement of Jerusalem Square by Valette Buildings and the erection of Darcy Buildings at London Fields, were the work of the more innovative London County Council. The LCC also, between the wars, built further new block estates at Stamford Hill and Whitmore Road, in the latter case moving the previous residents to Tottenham. The thirties saw increased activity in slum clearance by each of the boroughs, with building both on the cleared and fresh sites. Powell House at Lower Clapton notoriously replaced some of the finest eighteenth-century building in the area. The building of the LCC estate at Shore Place was interrupted by the last war. Woodberry Down was initiated as a major contribution to resolving the problem of the East End's slums, and at first was resisted and resented by Stoke Newington.

The separate boroughs created in 1900 to replace the old vestry system lasted until 1965, when they were reunited, together with the Borough of Shoreditch, to form the present London Borough of Hackney.

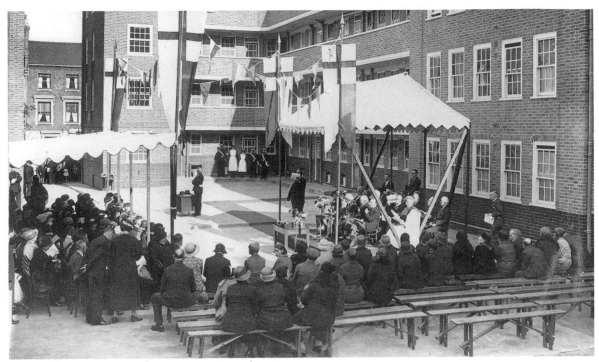

165. *The official opening of Stoke Newington Borough Council's Lordship House in 1934.*

166. *Hackney Baths, Lower Clapton Road, c1910.*

167. General Fleetwood, who lived at Fleetwood House.

Famous Names

Most of Stoke Newington's famous names are literary. Daniel Defoe (c1660-1730) was not only a student here – he lived successively at Newington Green and at Church Street. The title for his most famous work is perhaps an echo of the name of another pupil at Morton's academy – Timothy Cruso. Defoe's financial interests were precarious. At Newington Green he farmed civet cats (for their value in perfume manufacture), but his financial dealings ended in litigation with his mother-in-law.

Newington Green was the childhood home of the philosopher, John Stuart Mill, from 1810 for three years. The poet, Samuel Rogers (1763-1855), was brought up in a house on the Green; here, also, Mary Wollstonecraft and her sister set up a short-lived school. As a child in the 1820s the author of *Black Beauty*, Anna Sewell, lived in a country setting near what is now Palatine Avenue. Amongst less remembered writers, Anna Laetitia Barbauld and her niece Lucy Aikin, regaled later eighteenth and early nineteenth century dissenters with historical works and poetry. In Church Street was born the poet and historian, Isaac D'Israeli, father of Benjamin; and Edgar Allan Poe was a schoolboy at Dr Bransby's school. Lordship Terrace was home to the leading horticultural journalist Shirley

Hibberd, who was highly influential in promoting ideas of garden design and ornamentation among the Victorian middle classes.

James Brooks (1825-1902), the church architect, is amongst Stoke Newington's other noteworthy residents. He was architect of St Chad's, in Dunloe Street, Shoreditch, and the superb St Columba's in Kingsland Road. The least endangered of Brooks's Hackney buildings must be his own private residence at 42 Clissold Crescent. Hackney can claim the apprenticeship of George Gilbert Scott, who spent several years of pupilage in the 1820s learning his craft with James Edmeston in Brooksby's Walk.

Sir Thomas Sutton, founder of Charterhouse and said to have been the richest man in England of his time, is commemorated in the name of Sutton House (as well as in the central character of Ben Jonson's *Volpone*). The house's association with Sutton appears to have arisen because it was assumed, when the National Trust acquired the house in 1938, that it had something to do with him, whereas he owned the neighbouring plot of land to the west (and so is quite fittingly remembered in the name of Sutton Place). Sutton died in Hackney, but also had a strong association with Stoke Newington. In 1582 he married Elizabeth Dudley, widow of the rich brewer who held Stoke Newington manor from St Paul's, who is herself commemorated in a tomb in old St Mary's. For its part, Sutton House has its own literary association, with the Victorian novelist Lord Lytton, who was briefly a schoolboy here, while the premises were divided and housed a boys' boarding academy.

Hackney has been more remarkable for philanthropists than writers, though we have already noted it was where Celia Fiennes settled in her old age, and the interpreter of the Jewish East End, Israel Zangwill, lived at 113 Victoria Park Road. As well as the classic *The King of Schnorrers* he was a practitioner of the new school of fiction, the detective story. Stoke Newington is associated with Isaac Watts, but Hackney has its own hymn-writer in the shape of James Edmeston the architect, author of 'Lead, kindly light'. John Howard, the prison reformer, was born at a house on Lower Clapton Road. Howard is an example of many natives of Hackney whose association with the area is as a place of birth which did not long remain a place of residence: others include the martyred American War of Independence captain, John André, and the archaeologist Sir Leonard Woolley 'of Ur'.

Howard was far from the only philanthropist associated with our area. Catherine and William Booth, founders of the Salvation Army, lived in

168. *Sir Thomas Sutton, founder of Charterhouse.*

169. *Mary Wollstonecraft.*

170. *Israel Zangwill*

171. *Colonel John Okey, who was executed for his part in the trial of Charles I, lived in Barber's Barn, a house on the east side of Mare Street, south of where Darnley Road now runs.*

172. *Samuel Rogers.*

173. *James Brooks.*

174. *Laetitia Barbauld.*

175. *Sir George Gilbert Scott, by George Richmond.*

176. Catherine Booth.

177. John Howard.

178. 'General' William Booth.

Cambridge Lodge Villas, on the present site of St Joseph's Hospice, where Catherine was so disturbed by the bells. They moved to Gore Road, to a house since demolished, then to Clapton Common and Rookwood Road. Samuel Morley lived for many years at Craven Lodge, Stamford Hill. Dr Barnardo brought his family to the Cedars, a detached villa in Banbury Road bought for them by his father-in-law. Whether Dr Robert Knox (1793-1862), the anatomist notorious for purchasing cadavers from Burke and Hare in Edinburgh, was a philanthropist is a question more open than his Scottish contemporaries would have allowed. Ostracised in Scotland and cold-shouldered by the London medical establishment, he set up a moderately successful practice in what is now Exmouth Place, and a home at 46 Cassland Road; and here he died.

The Inner City

AN OVERSPILL SUBURB

In each century Hackney has seen migration from the City. By the 1880s, the pressure of numbers moving outwards was from manual workers leaving Whitechapel and Bethnal Green. They were joined later by Jewish refugees from Russia and the Baltic states who had settled in London in the 1880s. Gradually, middle-class Hackney, which had long regarded 'the East End' as something like foreign territory, found itself labelled by the rest of the world firmly as part of East London, although Stoke Newington has never seen itself as anything other than North London.

By the 1880s Hackney and Clapton had ceased to be fashionable. Better communications to more outlying areas had at once made it possible for the comfortably off to live further afield, and, in the form of railway-building, wreaked physical havoc on the Hackney streetscape. The old, large houses, which once accommodated well-to-do families and their servants, were now unwanted. In Cambridge Heath, Clapton and Upper Homerton their grounds were sub-divided for building, since the style of architecture was unappealing to the late Victorian eye and their size was burdensome to the late Victorian purse. The nineteenth-century villas of Stoke Newington and Dalston, however, and the surroundings of the Downs and of Victoria Park, have always retained the cachet which their developers intended them to have.

The population peaked in 1911, and has declined ever since.

179. Part of Brooke House after its first bombing in 1940.

POST-WAR YEARS

Extensive damage in the Second World War, which also claimed more than 700 civilian lives, heralded further clearance and rebuilding, some of which has taken half a century to achieve.

The post-war years have undoubtedly seen mistakes, most of them in the name of municipal improvement. The process of removing some of them, in the shape of unloved and defective tower blocks, began with the demolition of Northaird Point on the GLC's Trowbridge Estate at Hackney Wick in 1985.

Although poverty and unacceptable living conditions persist, Hackney does not fully deserve its label as a paradigm of inner city decay, which the 1980s attempted to confer on it. Different cultures, with their roots in the Mediterranean, the Middle and near East and the Caribbean, have brought with them a new lease of life for old buildings and neighbourhoods as homes for a new range of flourishing communities and religious groups. Furthermore, Hackney has been rediscovered by a new generation of the middle-class, as grateful as their City-employed forebears for the greenery and the tracts of Georgian and Victorian housing at an easy distance from Bishopsgate. They are determined to conserve them. Much of what is pleasurable about living in the present borough is owed to the Hackney Society, one of London's most conscientious and effective local amenity groups.

The moving out of small industries from workshops and warehouses has created scope for what is said to be Europe's largest population of artists. The Hackney Empire keeps its traditions alive, encouraging innovation, and Sutton House and the Round Chapel have been rescued from years of neglect and the threat of inappropriate redevelopment, for restoration and community use, through the commitment of local people. Many of these are resident through choice rather than chance. Hackney is still, as the late Sir John Betjeman found it, 'full of life and enterprise'.

180. The Britannia pub, Mare Street (later the 'Samuel Pepys'), after bombing in 1940.

181. *House in St Thomas's Square, before demolition in 1951.*

182. *The first, unsuccessful attempt to demolish Northaird Point, on the Trowbridge estate, in 1985.*